"I read your journal last evening, a great piece of writing with an exceptional amount of research. I do not think Big Fred will be offended if I referred to him as being older than some rocks in the parking lot. Thanks again for a great book. (Yesterday was my first day in physical therapy for my hamstring pull; they said that I did a good job on it.)
—Norm

"I can't begin to tell you how much I admire the way you have improved during this season. Whereas a lot of these guys just sort of shuffle off to Buffalo, you, on the other hand, are always upbeat, giving 150 percent, and making every effort to win the flippin' ball game. That's my kind of guy."
—Maury

"I love it! I am hooked. And...a comment on Maury—he is ageless, and I have played with him two different seasons. Did you know that he did not play two years ago— he took time out to have a total hip replacement. It is amazing that he has that much agility with that procedure and his age combined. He is my idol."
—Joe Raabe, former league president

Aslow-pitch summer

A slow-pitch summer

MY ROOKIE SENIOR SOFTBALL SEASON

Leon Speroff, M.D.
Professor of Obstetrics and Gynecology
Oregon Health & Science University

arnica
CREATIVE

Portland, Oregon

Library of Congress Cataloging-in-Publication Data

Speroff, Leon, 1935-
  A slow-pitch summer : my rookie senior softball season / Leon Speroff.
     p. cm.
  Includes bibliographical references.
  ISBN 978-0-9745686-9-0 (alk. paper)
  1. Softball for older people. 2. Softball for older people--Oregon--Portland--Anecdotes. I. Title.

GV881.25.S64 2007
796.357'8--dc22

                    2006100888

Advil® is a registered trademark of the Wyeth Consumer Healthcare.
A2000™ glove is a registered trademark of the Wilson brand.
"Cooper" bats are a product of KR3 Custom Bats.
Easton Sports brand © Jas D. Easton, Inc.
EST™ is a registered trademark of the Worth brand.
Glove Loogie™ is a registered trademark of the Clenzoil Worldwide Corporation.
Glovolium™ is a registered trademark of the Rawlings brand.
"Havoc" is a product of the Easton Sports brand
Kevlar is a registered trademark of the E. I. du Pont de Nemours and Company.

Louisville Slugger® is a registered trademark of the Hillerich & Bradsby Co.
Playmaker™ is a registered trademark of the Rawlings brand.
Prodigy™ is a registered trademark of the Worth brand.
Rawlings® is a registered trademark of K2, Inc.
The Stan Musial glove is a model produced by Rawlings and sold in the Playmaker line.
Wilson® Sporting Goods Company is a registered trademark of Amer Sports.
Worth® is a registered trademark of K2, Inc.
3-in-One® oil is a registered trademark of the WD-40 Company.

Cover and interior design by Aimee Genter
Photography by Sen Speroff and Rick Schafer

This book may not be reproduced in whole or in part, by electronic or any other means
which exist or may yet be developed, without permission from:

3739 SE Eighth Ave, Suite 1
Portland, Oregon 97202
www.arnicacreative.com

Arnica books are available at special discounts when purchased in bulk for premiums and sales promotions,
as well as for fundraising or educational use. Special editions or bulk excerpts can also be created for specification. For details,
contact the Sales Director at the address above.

DEDICATION

In appreciation for their support and encouragement, and for some of the best lines in my journal, I dedicate this book to my 2006 teammates on Team No. 5 in the Vancouver-Metro Senior Softball Association:

Norm Burr	Age 71
Terry Calhoun	Age 64
Dick Colbeth	Age 68
Oren Floyd	Age 71
Bill Holbert	Age 63
Don Huffman	Age 67
Larry Matheson	Age 63
Tim Myers	Age 65
Fred Pegelow	Age 66
Fred Sandau	Age 77
Bill Teafatiller	Age 68
Frank Vincenzo	Age 65
Maury Wilson	Age 78

TABLE OF

CONTENTS

FOREWORD

When Leon Speroff invited me to contribute the foreword to this book, I wondered if I would find his journal of a season of slow-pitch softball compelling reading. Having recently published my book, *Use It or Lose It,* that addresses issues on aging, I certainly approve of men over age sixty energetically participating in a competitive softball league of their peers. These "geezer jocks" no doubt find that playing an active team sport helps them revive the lost emotions of shared triumphs and failures that were important in their younger years.

I was pleasantly surprised by Leon's journal, which I found both fascinating and uplifting. He is a writer whose informative, engaging and witty prose, sprinkled with humorous anecdotes, brought his "season" alive. Not only did I learn about the intricacies of the properties of bats and gloves, but more importantly, about the challenges of keeping muscles and sinews going after they want to stop. The highs from successful plays and victories, balanced by the mistakes, lost opportunities and defeats, all add to the richness of this story that shows it is never too late to rediscover talents buried in the past. This book is going to make you want to share the camaraderie of a team experience yourself.

--Peter Snell, Ph.D.

Running for New Zealand, Peter Snell won the Olympic gold medal for 800 meters in Rome, 1960, and gold medals in the 800 meters and 1000 meters at the Tokyo Olympics in 1964. Snell has held five individual world-record times in the distances of 800 meters, 800 yards, and one mile. He never lost a major race. At age thirty-four, Snell moved to the United States and earned a B.S. in Human Performance at the University of California, Davis, and a Ph.D. in Exercise Physiology at Washington State University. Currently he is Associate Professor of Medicine at the University of Texas Southwestern Medical Center in Dallas, where he is Director of the Human Performance Laboratory. Snell, named New Zealand's Athlete of the Twentieth Century, is an enthusiastic advocate of exercise for older individuals.

PROLOGUE

I was driving home from work one day in April and thinking about softball. The most popular participant sport in the United States is softball. It is estimated that 25 million people play regularly and 56 million play at least one game during a year.[1] Over 240,000 teams were registered with the Amateur Softball Association in 2006. For many summers I played fast-pitch softball in Ohio, on two teams, four games every week. Then later, I played at a very high level in the military at Vandenberg Air Force Base in California. But, that was thirty-nine years ago, and now I am seventy-one years old.

I missed playing softball. I missed the camaraderie of being part of a team. I missed infield practice. Of course, I missed the competition, but I even missed the little things. I liked wearing a uniform, and I liked it that my mother always made sure it was clean for each game. I liked to carry my cleats, tied by the shoestrings, looped over my shoulder. I always enjoyed playing a late evening game under the lights; late enough for the dew to accumulate on the grass, making the grass sparkle and creating a special freshness and smell. So I thought: *Well . . . do something about it!*

I called the Portland Metro park system and inquired about old men's softball teams. I was given the names and phone numbers of three men; I left a message with each. Two of them called back. The Portland teams pleasantly informed me that I was way past the deadline for applications, and the teams were already full. But I was graciously invited to a practice for the 70-plus touring team of old men that travels once a month to play in weekend tournaments involving four games.

I was now excited and committed. I went to a sporting goods store. The rack held over fifty baseball gloves. Looking around and finding that I had the baseball section of the store to myself, I borrowed a softball from the next aisle, and pounded it into glove after glove. Looking at the prices, I knew it would be best to get this decision right. I finally settled on a *Prodigy* by Worth, for $100. I searched for glove oil, and I found the old, familiar Rawlings *Glovolium* that I used in my youth, only now it is a gel in a small jar.

The "cleats" were on a large table smack in the middle of a wide aisle. The thought occurred to me that it wouldn't look good to have an older man sitting on the floor trying on baseball shoes. So I picked six pairs with plastic cleats (no metal cleats allowed in the old men's league), moved to a small out-of-the-way aisle, sat on the floor to put the shoes on, and then clacked up and down the aisle. I kept thinking: I wish my equipment had been this good when I was younger. I picked the $35 Nike shoes. What a pleasant hour and a half!

My first baseball mitt was not a whole lot larger than my hand. The fingers were not tied together. There was no padding except for a roll of cloth that extended around the heel of the glove to the fifth finger. This padding formed the small pocket. Playing shortstop, I used that chocolate-brown glove for four years until it was falling apart. I bought my next glove, the famous Rawlings *Playmaker*, with the money I had earned on my paper route. The PM 1 was a little too expensive for me, so I paid $18.50 for a PM 2. The *Playmaker* had only three fingers (you put your index and second fingers in the finger next to the webbing). A shaped hinge pad formed a "deep well" pocket. I loved that glove, and I cried three years later when I lost it (apparently it fell unknowingly out of my father's car).

Gloves were first used in baseball in the 1870s.[2] Padding was added a decade later. Until then, bruised and broken fingers were the norm, especially among catchers. The early gloves, therefore, were worn for protection, but even these barely adequate coverings improved fielding. The Rawlings *Playmaker* top-of-the-line was the PM, the Stan Musial model, that laced the fingers together for the first time around 1950, and for the first time, baseball gloves didn't look like a hand. The modern era in baseball gloves began in 1957 when Wilson Sporting Goods introduced the model A2000, with flattened, thinner fingers and thumb (not thick and roundish like previous gloves), and with the thumb beginning further up on the palm and reaching up as far as the fingers, producing a better pocket and an effective web for trapping the ball.[3] Beginning in the 1950s, the gloves were hinged at the bottom of the fifth finger, making it easier to close the mitt around the ball. The outer margins of the modern mitts adopted a diagonal shape to further enhance the pocket, in contrast to the rectangular shape of the older gloves. It was finally recognized that the baseball mitt should not mimic the appearance of a hand, but rather it should enhance the movements of a hand in catching a ball. The modern glove catches the ball where your hand isn't.[4] In recent years, ballplayers have put their index fingers out of the gloves, which produces less bruising to be sure, but more importantly, the glove can more easily close at its hinge, and gloves are now made with appropriate openings. I'm old school—I like all fingers enclosed.

Practice was on Wednesday, so the previous weekend I went to a batting cage. I hit 200 balls on the slow-pitch softball machine. I started out with vim and vigor, but progressively between token insertions for another ten balls, my rest periods became longer and soon I was leaning over with my hands braced on the fencing to catch my breath. But, encouraged by periodic line drives, I said, *"I can do this!"*

From the batting cage, I went back to the sporting goods store. I had to have batting gloves. Aluminum bats were a new experience for me; they vibrate and they sting. Returning to a now familiar part of the store, I was pleased to again find myself alone. I tried on six different pairs of gloves, deciding on the $25 Easton gloves with the "vibration-reduction-system." I was ready.

Ted Williams, arguably baseball's greatest hitter, said that when he hit the ball square he could see the stitches on the ball just before he hit it. That happened to me once when I hit the only home run in my life. The 392nd Aerospace Medical Squadron was playing on the beautiful main field at Vandenberg Air Force Base, a well-cared-for ballpark complete with stands and outfield fences. It was the last inning and we were losing 2 to 1. I knew I had hit the ball well, and immediately as I headed toward first base, I thought: that's what Ted Williams was talking about. I looked up in time to see the ball going over the left-field fence to tie the score. We lost in extra innings, but it was my magical moment.

The seemingly simple act of hitting a ball with an implement is actually a complicated exercise in physics. A ballplayer has to swing a bat with sufficient acceleration to strike a moving object that hardly ever follows the same path twice. Batters and fielders know a good hit from the feel of the impact and the cracking sound of a wooden bat or, with aluminum, the pinging sound. Recreational hitters don't spend any time analyzing the forces involved; natural ability is allowed free rein and the best hitters benefit from inherent talent—a good combination of strength, visual acuity, and coordination. Not many of us can swing the bat so that the ball repeatedly hits the center of percussion, the "sweet spot" of the bat.

Sweet spot is an apt name. When a ball is hit in this spot, it really feels good. Simplifying the physics, a bat has a center of percussion, the spot on the bat when hit by a ball, where the forces applied to a batter's hands are neutralized and there is no energy directed to move the bat under the hands.[5] All the force is aimed at the ball and any sensation in the hands is minimized. But it is more complicated: the center of percussion is not always in the same location because the pivot point of the bat varies; thus, the sweet spot is not in the same exact spot swing after swing, and varies from batter to batter.[3]

The mysteries of batting have attracted the attention of scientists mainly due to the development of durable, high-performance aluminum bats.[6-12] We have learned that the most critical element in good hitting is bat speed. For this reason, a lighter-weight bat is now recommended. The advantage of a greater hitting mass in a heavier bat is more than lost by the slower speed of a heavy bat.[5] Major league baseball bats averaged forty ounces in weight in the 1920s, and today the bats average thirty-two ounces.[7] It is just too hard to swing a heavy bat fast enough, and in addition, the lighter bats provide a small, but important, increase in reaction time and bat control (the ability to hit balls in different locations as they cross the plate).

Most of the wooden bats used in professional baseball are made from *Fraxinus americana*, the northern white ash that grows in Pennsylvania and New York. The best bats come from trees that are at least forty-five years old, with six to ten rings per inch.[7] It is increasingly difficult to find this quality of white ash, threatening the future existence of this icon of baseball. Professional ballplayers have insisted on increasingly skinny handles to allow greater bat speed, a change that leads to more broken bats and more wood consumption. Major league baseball teams use a total of about 180,000 bats per season, 70 percent from Louisville Slugger and the rest divided among Rawlings, Worth, and Cooper.[7] Once adjusted, automatic lathes can produce a bat in a few minutes; special custom models require twenty minutes and a hand-operated lathe.

Softball and amateur baseball players use only aluminum bats. Cost varies with performance quality, from $20 to $400. Competition among the bat manufacturers produced lighter and lighter models with greater and greater performance capabilities. Batting averages and home runs increased, exemplified by the score in the 1998 Division I collegiate title game, 21–14, Southern California over Stanford. The hollow aluminum bats could be a little wider without sacrifice in weight, achieving greater bat speed and a larger sweet spot. Good hits are more frequent with balls hit closer to the handle or to the end of the bat because of the larger sweet spot. A thirty-four-inch aluminum bat weighs two to four ounces lighter than a wooden bat of the same length.[7] Most slow-pitch aluminum bats weigh twenty-six to twenty-nine ounces; fast-pitch softball bats are even lighter. An aluminum bat is particularly suited for slow-pitch softball where you have to wait longer for the ball to get to you. An aluminum bat requires less time to swing, allowing a late decision.

A good batter doesn't choose a bat just by reading the weight listed on the knob of the bat. The key is the "feel" when swinging a bat. Some light bats can feel heavier on a swing than a heavy bat, or, said in a different way, two bats weighing the same can feel very different when they are swung.[5] This is known as the "swing weight."

The arms and hands transfer energy to the bat, which is generated by the rotation of the body and the lateral movement of the torso accomplished by stepping into the ball.[13] The rapidity of the rotation of a bat around the wrists is the major contributing factor to bat speed. The average pivot point is actually about 2.5 inches beyond the knob of the bat and about 2.5 inches below the axis of the bat, but this point varies from batter to batter and even from swing to swing for each batter.[5] The swing weight of a bat is determined by its moment of inertia, the force to be overcome in order to achieve a bat speed.[5] The lower the moment of inertia, the faster a bat can be swung. This force is influenced by the balance point of the bat, which is the location where a bat would balance on an edge. Differences in balance points cause variations in the moment of inertia. Hence, bats of similar weights can feel different to a batter. The closer the balance point is to the handle of the bat, the easier it is to swing. Strong individuals can produce a greater collision efficiency with a higher moment of inertia because of more weight toward the end of the bat, as long as they can maintain the same swing speed provided by a lighter bat. A timing mismatch, measured in hundredths of a second, spoils a good hit.

> There is an **art** to batting, expressed in the infinite individual variations in batting stances and swings.

The key is to achieve good bat speed with maximum wrist rotation using a bat that "feels good." Okay, we have always known that. Pick up one bat after another, and use the one that feels good. It's not just science. There is an art to batting, expressed in the infinite individual variations in batting stances and swings.

The aluminum alloys (zinc-magnesium-aluminum) used for bats originated in the aerospace industry, allowing great strength despite thin walls. Newer alloys incorporate a small amount of copper for added strength. The hollow bats are filled with a substance to deaden the sound, usually polyurethane foam or cork. One would think this structure would allow a trampoline effect, the wall indenting and then springing back to add to the impact, but some experts have concluded that the collision of a ball and bat is too short in duration to allow such an effect, and furthermore, the aluminum bats are too strong to react in such a manner; others disagree and attribute some of the performance to this effect.[5]

The durability of an aluminum bat is a major factor in its dominance of the nonprofessional market, but it doesn't last forever. The aluminum eventually becomes fatigued, after two to five seasons in a typical college schedule.[7] Bat manufacturers are now producing composite bats, incorporating ceramic, scandium, Kevlar fibers, or graphite fibers. The goal is to sound like a wooden bat and perform even better than an aluminum bat.

Aluminum bat technology was too good; super performance soon came to be viewed as a potential danger, producing batted balls with exceptional speed. Organizations such as the National Collegiate Athletic Association (NCAA) adopted regulations that established limits for barrel sizes, length, and weight. Titanium bats, stronger and lighter than aluminum, were banned. The objective is to produce a good bat, but also to limit performance according to guidelines established by governing bodies such as the International Softball Federation, the Amateur Softball Association, and the United States Specialty Sports Association (which prior to 1997, was the U.S. Slo-Pitch Softball Association, USSSA). Now bats must pass standardized laboratory tests measuring the ratio of ball speeds after and before collision with a stationary bat (collision speed ratio) and measuring the coefficient of restitution.

When a ball collides with a bat, the ball is compressed. This deformation is greater with a softball compared with a baseball.[5] The speed of a ball is less after being hit, an effect measured by the coefficient of restitution (a ratio calculated by dividing the speed at which a ball bounces back by the speed the ball is thrown at a wall—speed after a collision divided by the speed before collision). Softballs are constructed to have a coefficient of restitution of 0.44 when the speed of the pitch is sixty miles per hour, compared with 0.55 for a baseball and a pitch of ninety miles per hour.[5]

Dividing the collision speed ratio (a joint property of bat and ball) by the coefficient of restitution ratio (property of only the ball) produces a new ratio, the Bat Performance Factor (BPF). The governing bodies of softball set a maximal limit of 1.20 for the BPF. However, bats can be made that pass the BPF test, but still have super performance because of shifts in balance points and the location of moment of inertia. A new standard was developed for softball that uses a higher speed for the balls and scans the impact locations on individual bats, isolating the location of maximal performance. The bats are then tested at this location.

The ball used in baseball has changed little since 1872 when a weight of 5 to 5.25 ounces and a circumference of 9 to 9.25 inches were established.[14,15] Early baseballs were made by wrapping yarn around a melted rubber center, topped by sewing on a leather cover. In 1910, the rubber center was replaced by cork, an idea taken from the ball used in cricket. A layer of rubber surrounds the cork to prevent swelling or shrinkage. A change in 1931 created the ball still used today: a small sphere of cushioned cork, composed of rubber and cork, is enclosed by two pieces of black rubber, sealed by red rubber gaskets, and surrounded by an outer layer of red rubber. For the 600,000 major league baseballs used each year, the cushioned cork and rubber center of a baseball is produced by the Muscle Shoals Rubber Company in Batesville, Mississippi. Cowhide covers produced at the Tennessee Tanning Company in Tullahoma, Tennessee, replaced horsehide in 1974. After machine wrapping the core with three layers of wool (121 yards of thicker gray wool yarn, forty-five yards of thinner white yarn and fifty-three yards of thin gray yarn) and one outer layer of 150 yards of fine polyester/cotton yarn, the cover of a baseball is cemented to the wound ball. Eighty-eight inches of waxed red thread is hand-sewed in thirteen to fourteen minutes, bringing the two figure-eight-shaped pieces of the cover together with 108 stitches. The seams are rolled with a machine to compress the surface and produce a uniform surface. Statistically representative balls are tested to meet the standards for the coefficient of restitution and compression. Yarns used for balls are stored under controlled temperature and humidity conditions and wound under constant tension. The objective is uniformity.

Softballs are not soft, but they are not the same as baseballs because there is no yarn wrapping. A solid polyurethane core is covered with two stitched pieces of cowhide, which is either white or bright yellow in color for high visibility (it's called "optic yellow"). The ball weighs 6.6 ounces, and the circumference of the ball is twelve inches. Modern softballs come in different coefficient of restitution ratios; the higher the number the farther they travel. The Vancouver-Metro Senior Softball Association deliberately chose to use balls with a 0.44 ratio, a lower ratio to reduce the risk of injuries from a batted ball. Now I know more about bats and balls than when I played as a boy and young man.

Softball began by accident on a November day in Chicago, in 1887.[16,17] Yale and Harvard alumni were at the Farragut Boat Club waiting for a Western Union messenger to report the score of the Harvard-Yale football game. One Yalie, excited when he learned that Yale was victorious by a score of 17–8, picked up an old boxing glove and threw it at a nearby alumnus of Harvard who tried to hit it back with a stick. George Hancock, a reporter for the Chicago Board of Trade, said, "Let's play baseball." The boxing glove with tightly tied laces became the ball, and a home plate, pitcher's box, and bases were chalked on the gymnasium floor of the Boat Club. It was a close game; the final score was 41–40. The Farragut team challenged other gyms for indoor games, and in the spring the games moved to the outdoors. Hancock drafted the first rules for what was called indoor-outdoor baseball. The rules were officially adopted by the Mid-Winter Indoor Baseball League of Chicago in 1889. The game spread throughout the Midwest, becoming very popular in Minneapolis.

In Minneapolis, Louis Rober, an official in the fire department, fostered the game to keep his men occupied and moved it outdoors. By 1895, the game was being called Kitten Ball after Rober's team, the Kittens. In 1925, the Minneapolis Park Board changed the name to Diamond Ball, and in 1926, Walter Hakanson, director of the Denver YMCA, suggested the name, Softball, first in Colorado and then to the various rules committees. In 1933, teams throughout America were organized into city and state organizations, largely through the efforts of Leo Fischer, a sports writer for the *Chicago American*, and Michael J. Pauley, a Chicago sporting goods salesman. The sport received large-scale publicity when fifty-five teams were invited by Fischer and Pauley to participate in a tournament associated with the 1933 World's Fair in Chicago. The Amateur Softball Association was formed in 1933, providing structure and organization to the game, which at first was exclusively fast pitch, but now over 90 percent of the adult participants play slow-pitch softball.

19 APRIL

My first practice was at 11 AM, so I left home at 10. The field was at Delta Park, a large area near the Columbia River with multiple well-cared-for softball fields, all with a great up-river view of Mount Hood. It was a special feeling to walk on a manicured softball diamond again. The guys were members of the Portland 70-plus touring team. For two hours we had batting practice and caught the balls hit by the batters. I did not distinguish myself.

I counted the fly balls. Sixteen came my way, and I dropped six. The very first ball was coming right to me. I raised my mitt to catch the ball in front of my face, and the ball went by, about six inches to the left of the mitt. *What is this? I thought I had it!* It soon became apparent that catching a fly ball is harder than it used to be.

> It soon became **apparent** that catching a fly ball is **harder** than it used to be.

The easier balls to catch are those to one side or the other, when without thinking, you can tell almost immediately that the ball is off to the side, and you quickly make your move. Ball players have always recognized that the ball hit straight at an outfielder is the most difficult to judge. It takes a critical two seconds to judge a straight ball because the initial rate of rise doesn't reveal how far the ball is going to go.[18] Less experienced and less skillful outfielders take longer, and often, it is too late.

I have observed a new outfield problem, one associated with aging. When you camp under a fly and wait for the ball, you are totally focused on the ball. I quickly perceived that at my age, you depend a lot on your total field of vision for balance. Waiting for a fly ball, vision concentrated on that small object, balance becomes a problem. *Things wobble!!!*

My hitting wasn't bad. The secret to hitting a slowly pitched softball is having patience for the ball to arrive, and timing it just right. Hitting ten in a row, I found that my first swings yielded line drives, but as I tired, I began to hit dribblers.

The guys were great, shouting encouragement, reminding me that it takes a while to get back in the groove. Some of these guys play over one hundred games every summer, on multiple teams. I came home a little discouraged, wondering if I could match up. Furthermore, I had pulled my left hamstring, and was hobbled for about three days.

20 APRIL

I received an email telling me that the traveling tourney team from Vancouver, just across the Columbia River, was practicing on Thursday April 27th at noon, and I was also assigned to Team No. 5 in the 60-plus Vancouver league.

27 APRIL

I went to the softball diamond on the campus of Clark College for practice with the Vancouver 70-plus team. This experience was much better. My hitting was still pretty good, and I didn't miss any fly balls.

This time I pulled my left quadriceps, but not severely, only two days of discomfort. I also discovered that my work schedule would allow me to make only two of the five trips with the team. I decided to stick with Team No. 5, playing on weeknights, and no traveling.

I called Bill, the coach of Team No. 5, and told him I had been assigned to his team. We had a good time talking, as I warned him I hadn't played for many years. He put me at ease, telling me about his first fly ball when he came back to play, which hit him in the face and gave him a bloody nose. We closed with him telling me, "Come to practice Saturday and I will evaluate you."

29 APRIL

Nervous!! The idea of trying out under the watchful eye of the managing coach was very unsettling. Driving to the practice, I found myself very anxious, even shaking a little with tension. I was so nervous; I forgot to put my batting gloves on my first time in the batter's box. When I got home and took a shower, I thought I had dirt on my right

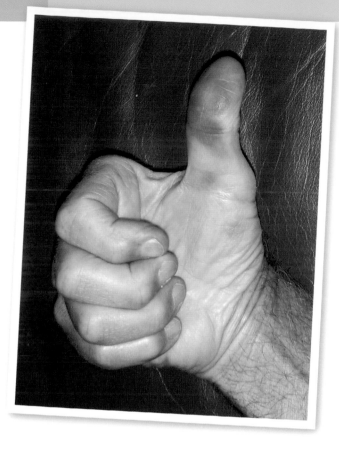

thumb, but it wouldn't scrub off. My right thumb was black and blue from aluminum bat vibrations, a convincing argument to use batting gloves, especially mine with the "vibration-reduction system."

At the practice, as with my previous two sessions, the No. 5 guys were very engaging, helpful, and pleasant. I wonder if they select their playing outfits with as much careful attention as I do. I wear a softball, three-quarter-arm-length jersey under a T-shirt. Thus far, I have worn an Ohio State shirt, a gray Cleveland Browns shirt, and today an orange Browns shirt. The shirts I see on the field vary from T-shirts with logos to polo shirts. My favorite today: a light blue T-shirt on a pot-bellied (a small one) man that reads: "Aches and Pains." One of the best hitters wears a light jersey with "Dakota's Bar & Grill, Shautenberg, Illinois" on the back, and on the front: "Geezers Softball League."

The hats are a motley collection. A variety of major league baseball caps, one from the Western Telephone Service, another proclaiming Northwest Pipe Company, and mine, featuring Estancia de Los Rios Fly Fishing Lodge (in Chile). My wife asked if we had uniforms. I said, "Only the traveling tournament team has uniforms." She wondered how we could tell which team was which, did one wear shirts and one not? (We used to call it "shirts and skins" when we played pickup basketball games.) I pointed out that one team was in the field and the other was at bat. "Clever," she said.

Being brand new, my mitt is stiff as a board, but it is getting better. I have worked and worked with it to gain some softness. Over one jar of *Glovolium* has been rubbed in. My equestrian daughter recommended a French oil used for new saddles, and I have used a half bottle. I have pounded it and pounded it, heated it with a hair dryer, and left it sitting in sunshine. But still an occasional ball hits it and bounces out (it can't be all my fault!).

Breaking in a mitt has two objectives: to soften the leather, making the glove flexible, and to form a pocket. The pocket is the right spot to

I have **pounded it** and **pounded it,** heated it with a hair dryer, and left it sitting in sunshine.

catch a ball, centered just below the index finger. Gloves, with their thick leather, have to be stiff when new because the breaking-in process is geared to molding the glove to the owner's hand. Even the internal padding gradually fits the hand.

Yogi Berra put his new mitts in the whirlpool until the mitt stopped bubbling. Then he dried the mitt out for two or three days in the clothes dryer.[19] Many ballplayers pound the hell out of a mitt with a baseball bat; others just start using a new mitt in practice until it is ready. A good layer of oil is important, with a little extra in the pocket and hinge, but the experts agree: repeated oiling is unnecessary and unhealthy for the leather. Then go to it: pounding and pounding on the leather in the pocket, kneading the base of the web where it is attached and the hinge where there are multiple layers of leather. The mitt improves with every catch and every pound of the throwing hand.

In the old days, players used neatsfoot oil made from boiling the leg bones of cows (no longer recommended because it stiffens with time), vaseline (doesn't penetrate the leather), mink oil (hardens at room temperature), saddle soap (a soap, not an oil), linseed oil (makes leather stiff), and even shaving cream (contains no lanolin).[20] Some players oil their gloves and bake them for a few minutes in an oven. In my youth I used *3-In-One* oil (too thick and permanent) and used a rope to tie my glove with a ball in it overnight. Now it's a commercial special lanolin product and a bungee cord. There is no substitute for pounding the glove hundreds of times with a ball or your fist. I noticed at practice that I was the only one with a new glove, and the only one constantly pounding his fist into the mitt. My brother Ted tells me to put the mitt under a tire and run over it back and forth; he swears Cal Ripken used this method. I am not going to run over my new mitt with my car!

I decide to try *Glove Loogie* and order it over the internet from the Clenzoil Corporation in Westlake, Ohio (near Cleveland). I grew up in Ohio and I am still fanatical about the Cleveland Browns (I have season tickets) and the Cleveland Indians (I even occasionally go to spring training). My *Glove Loogie* comes in the mail, and I am delighted to learn that the Cleveland Indians have been using *Glove Loogie* for five years and love it. The company president, Jack FitzGerald, wrote me a personal note, thanking me for my business. Apparently, the Ohio company

discovered the *Glove Loogie* formula (still a secret, but it contains a powerful penetrating agent and petroleum distillate saturated with lanolin) "almost by accident, while doing research for another project." After a feature in *Playboy* magazine (I wonder how that happened) and a rave in *Sporting News*, business took off. If it's good enough for the Cleveland Indians, it's good enough for me. I am a convert to *Glove Loogie*.

At the end of hitting practice, four guys stayed to take infield practice. I decided to hang around, so I moved to the outfield to back them up for any missed balls. The hitter (Dakota's Bar & Grill) noticed me and began to include fly balls for me in the rotation around the field. He hit about fifteen balls to me and I caught them all except for three over my head and the very last one. I camped under the last one, and things wobbled; the ball bounced against my glove. I realized I was pooped, and I amazed myself by making the very rational decision to walk off the field.

At the end of practice, Coach Bill came over and said, "You did good out there. You can help us. Don't worry about missing a ball now and then. Catching two out of three will be good."

GAMES 1 & 2

Gameday! Opening ballgame! Actually, it's opening ballgames. Each time we play, it's a double header. The *Vancouver-Metro Senior Softball Association* was formed in 1994 for players age sixty and older. All league games are played on the softball diamond at Clark College in Vancouver, which is just across the Columbia River from Portland. Through an agreement with Clark College, the founding players improved an unused baseball field, and annual dues of $50 per player are used to provide supplies and to maintain the field.

Being a little anxious, I get to the field in time to watch the man paint the foul lines. The infield has been scraped into a circular pattern, and I notice a white line six feet to each side of second base, and two first-base bags; one is orange.

As the guys gathered, I learned about the special rules in our eight-team league, rules established to avoid collisions and protect old bodies. Trying to beat out a ground ball, you are required to tag the "safety base," the orange bag outside the foul line, abutting the regular first base bag, otherwise you are called out. Running to second base, you run outside the white lines on each side of the bag, and you don't need to touch the bag unless you are heading to third. Running to third, you can run past the bag. The home plate for scoring runs is eight feet to the side of the plate for batting. No sliding and no tags: each out at a base is a force-out. The "mercy" rule is five and out, a maximum of five runs can be scored in any inning but the last inning (the seventh inning). We play eleven fielders (four outfielders and a rover).

Early and late in the season, in order to finish two games before daylight is gone, each bat starts with a count of one and one. When the count is two strikes, a second foul ball is an out. Base runners cannot leave the bag until the ball crosses home plate, and there is no stealing. The dimensions of a slow-pitch softball field are a little different compared with fast-pitch softball, designed to slow the game down. The slow-pitch baselines are sixty-five feet in length compared with sixty feet in fast pitch, and the pitching distance is fifty feet compared with forty-six feet.

The pitcher throws a high, arcing ball with reverse spin. It is supposed to reach a high

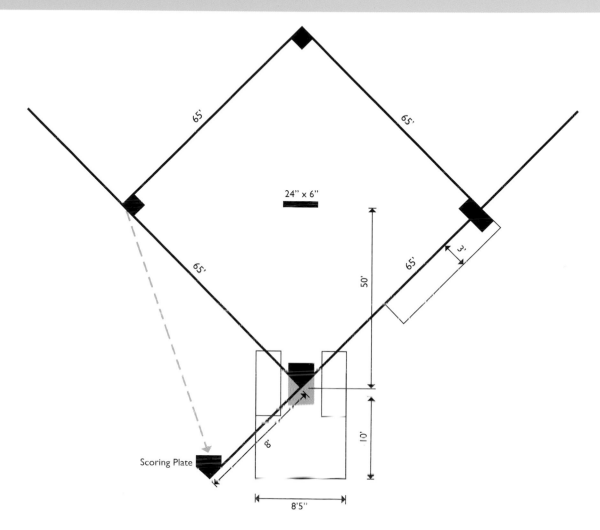

point of six-to-twelve feet from the ground. As I stood at the plate for the first time and watched the first pitch, my head moved up to look at the sky and then down to watch the ball bounce on the plate; "Strike!" said the umpire. Strikes are not horizontal with the ground! A ball that hits the plate (which is enlarged with a two-foot extension) is a strike. The strategy is simple: no waiting out the pitcher. When you see a pitch you think you can hit, go for it.

The lineup is posted on the fence. Each individual must play at least three innings, but everyone gets to bat. For opening day, we have twelve men and I am penciled in eleventh in the batting order and alternating innings with Fred in right field. Whoa! That is a blow to my ego. We always used to put the weakest person in right field. But Bill, our coach, says it will take a couple of games to shake the lineup out. Bill's attire is special. He has dark blue shorts on, but his legs are covered. White knee-length socks with purple stirrups match his white and purple jersey. His knees are covered with kneepads, one blue and one black.

What a forlorn feeling to have the team run on the field and be left sitting alone on the bench.

The team takes the field. Eleven fielders and it is not my turn to be in right field. This means that I am the only one left on the bench. What a forlorn feeling to have the team run on the field and be left sitting alone on the bench. Probably not many noticed because the stands (the lawn behind the fence) are only half full, but after a few innings, the other two people show up.

My first time up, I make it to first base when the third basemen mishandles my ground ball. I come around to score, and Terry, the retired high school teacher and basketball coach, yells, "Harder! You have to sprint." I give him an astonished look and shout,

"I was sprinting!" It makes me wonder what a scout for the National Football League would think of our times in the forty-yard dash; I'm not even sure anyone can "dash" forty yards.

Once again, I pulled a muscle, this time, my right quadriceps. I have been running since 1976. I used to go five miles at lunchtime; I ran in 10K and 15K races, and once, I ran a half-marathon. Those days are gone. Now I run two miles three times per week on a treadmill, then I pump iron. I have been working out with weights and machines for fifteen years. So why am I pulling hamstring and quadriceps muscles, near the attachments at the pelvis? The answer is acceleration. Every muscle pull occurred when I went from standing still to a run, accelerating as fast as I could. That obviously has never been part of my workouts. I'll have to practice going from standing still to full speed. *I wonder if anyone will notice the difference.*

The innings go by fast. Everyone is caught up in the spirit of the game, with chatter between pitches and compliments for nice plays. We even pull off a double play on a grounder to shortstop. We lose the first game 16–15, and win the second game 15–10. I bat five times in the two games and get four hits: two line drives, a grounder in the hole, and a little pop in the infield that shouldn't have been a hit, but fell in. My line in the box score looks terrific: four for five and five runs scored.

The high scores reflect some good hitting and a lot of poor fielding. But no errors for me! (Okay, I admit it, not a single ball came to me in the outfield.) I go home and take the two Advils that my wife had left out on the bathroom counter for me.

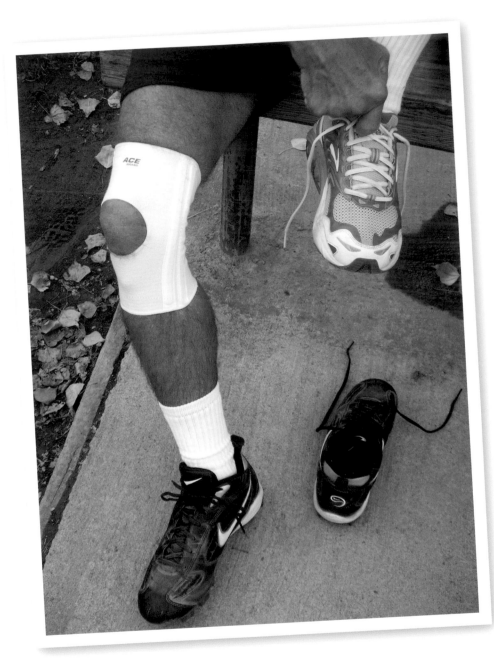

GAMES 3 & 4

Blasted... clobbered... crushed... drubbed... flattened... jolted... mauled... pounded... pummeled... rocked... routed... smashed tattooed... trounced... walloped, and whipped.

We lost both games, 18–3 and 21–12. It was one of those days when almost everything we hit went right to someone (and they were good fielders), and many of their hits were falling between our guys. Our only bright spot was Oren's grand slam home run over the left fielder's head in the second game. I was "promoted" to seventh in the batting order and to right center in the field, but I was a sad one for six; my best hit of the night would easily have sailed over the left fielder; however, it was foul by *inches*.

Only three guys are older than I am; the rest range in age from sixty-three to seventy-one. Every single member of our team wants to win, enjoys winning. But I notice that winning takes second place to just playing. We all have the same problem: diminished strength and stamina. We can't run as fast as we used to. We can't throw hard and far. And we all have trouble bending over quickly. But playing is a statement, a challenge to aging. Each and every one of us is grateful to be here, to be able to play senior softball, even with its slower pace and special rules.

I have had two surgeries, one on the right foot and one on the left foot, both to repair anatomical changes incurred over time from running. The recovery each time was painful in the short-term and slow in the rehabilitation. To be able to run pain-free is a tribute to my orthopedic surgeon. At my age and after my orthopedic procedures, it is a joy to be alive and running on a ball field. As we left the field at the end of the second game, I pointed out that it was a moral victory; we were still alive.

Fred is seventy-seven years old. He is dressed very professionally for today's games: real baseball pants with blue stirrup socks and a blue baseball jersey. Fred is a real hero in my book; throughout his working life, he taught in the Portland schools, students in the fourth, fifth, and sixth grades. He emphasizes that his rewards came from the kids, not from the parents and not from the administrators. Fred is a big man. I call him Big Fred. Not overweight at all, he is tall and husky with a Mediterranean darkness. He must have been an imposing teacher, until his innate kindness became apparent. Big Fred never paddled a student, but he enjoys telling us that one year his students made him a large paddle in shop class, which he hung prominently on the wall behind his desk. He has played softball all his life, fast pitch when young, and slow pitch for the last twenty years. He has played in national tournaments, and in 2000, his team won the senior's national championship.

Playing right field and first base for us, Fred has now slowed down, but he is strong and hits well. I often run for him when he reaches base. I thank Fred when I learn that he was instrumental in founding the coed and senior men's slow-pitch leagues in Vancouver.

Norm is total green. A green baseball cap tops a green shirt with number 16 on the back. His long pants are green,

Norm is **talkative,** something that probably comes in handy in his work. He has been in "labor management" for six decades.

and when he lifts his pants to put his cleats on, I see baseball socks with green stirrups. I am reluctant to ask him about the color of his underwear. Norm likes to catch, a good place for him as he shouts out instructions to his infielders and outfielders. Norm is talkative, something that probably comes in handy in his work. He has been in "labor management" for six decades. He now serves as a consultant. When a labor force in a small company wants to unionize, he is called on by management to convince the workers it is not a good choice. I didn't tell him that my father was a Marxist.

Our second baseman, Terry, is thin, wiry, and a little hyperactive. He is our cheerleader, and he likes to coach first base. I'm standing on first and he says, "The first three steps are critical. You have to get a quick start." Later, Terry is sitting on the bench massaging his left upper quadriceps with the side of a water bottle. "It's those first three steps, Terry."

In our second game, I had my chance to make a spectacular catch. PING, and I immediately knew it was a hard hit ball to my left. I turned and ran back; I looked up at the long drive that was sailing over my head; I lifted my glove, and A-R-R-R-R-G-G-G-H! The ball hit the top of my mitt and bounced away. I wanted that catch! I *really* wanted that catch!! I confess—I wanted the accolades of my teammates. A polite "nice try" does not equal an enthusiastic "great catch."

Coach Bill is a big-framed man, a little herky-jerky with an awkward throw, but he gets it done, playing first base and hitting some long balls. For today's games, Coach Bill is featuring the color red. A red baseball jersey is covered by a T-shirt that says "Rick's Custom Fencing & Decking" on the back. His lower legs are covered to the knees with bright red socks. This time both of his knee pads are black. Bill plays with a cholesterol of 300, and that is a decrease from 600, achieved with two medications. His lipid disorder carries an incredibly high risk of atherosclerosis and heart disease. He has never had a heart attack, and he knows that he is fortunate to be playing softball. Coach Bill says, "Our problem is team speed. All I can do is hope to put the guys in the right spot, then pray."

Just before going home, when we congregate at the bench, stowing our equipment, I ask the fellows, "Do you know what a nadir is?" Tim says, "Sure, it's the opposite of apogee." "Right," I say, "and this is our nadir, next is our apogee."

GAMES 5 & 6

It's unusually hot for May in Oregon, ninety-five degrees at game time and eighty-nine after the last out. But this is Oregon hot, not Ohio hot. Ohio hot is ninety/ninety: 90 degrees and 90 percent humidity. During the first game, I look at our team on the bench and not a single player is sweating. But we all use our water bottles frequently to compensate for the high loss of water from evaporation. I like the heat. I even liked Ohio heat, when dressed

in a full uniform with a dark color, soon you were soaking wet. Softball is a game meant to be played in hot weather; muscles seem to function easier and better, and hitting the ball is less like swinging a bat against a solid tree.

Norm is total green again. I screw up my courage and ask him, "What's the color of your underwear?" "Chartreuse," he says, but he is immediately overruled by Big Fred who yells out, "It's pink."

Maury is a marvel. At seventy-eight years of age, Maury is our oldest player. Short, thick-bodied and muscular, he has great reflexes, a requirement for him as our third baseman. Maury played fast-pitch softball as a shortstop throughout his twenty-year, Air Force career, after which he became the traffic safety director for the city of Portland. He played at the highest level; on one occasion he was a member of a military all-star team composed of the best players from all branches of the service. Maury slathers 45 SPF on so thickly his face and thighs are ghost white. He has played so much softball in the sunshine that he has had several skin lesions requiring treatment.

Bill, one of our pitchers, is a compact man with a gentle smile who seems on the quiet side until you get to talking with him. He grew up in Texas where he played all the sports in his small-town school that had 430 students in all twelve grades. Bill escaped Texas by joining the Army. After discovering the Pacific Northwest by marrying a woman from Washington, he worked as an electrician for twenty-seven years.

Coach Bill is in yellow today. "Not yellow; it's golden!" he corrects me. And golden it is, as Bill has six hits in seven at bats. Unfortunately, it is not enough as once more we lose a doubleheader, 9–7 in the first game and 14–6 in the second. Obviously it's too hot for an apogee. We can't come up with clutch hits and leave too many men on base, while in the field we give up runs by committing too many errors. There are a lot of hits in slow-pitch softball, but it is my early impression that games are won and lost on defense. There are no routine plays; every play is an adventure.

Dick is a bemedaled Vietnam veteran with 18 years of service in the Air Force coming after very difficult and rough years early in his life. He was never an athlete and insists on doing his own running because this is his first ever experience of getting on base. "The part I love the best is that many guys recognize that I don't fit in well; certainly I'm an athletic goof, and they go out of their way to tell me how wonderful I am if I accidentally make a play or get on base." During our game, Dick confesses, "I feel like an old man." "Hell," says Norm, "We're all old men. There are rocks out there younger than Fred."

I am very happy when there is a good interval between batted balls coming my way. I "sprint" after a ball, toss it to my relay man, and then walk to my position huffing and

I am hoping the other guys are having the same experience, and, like me, outwardly they act **cool, nonchalant** and **non-stressed.**

puffing. I definitely do not remember being grateful in my younger days for breathing time. I am hoping the other guys are having the same experience, and, like me, outwardly they act cool, nonchalant and non-stressed. Terry, our second basemen, moves to the outfield in the late innings of the second game. He says, "Wow, this is a long way out here. How do you old guys do it every inning?" I answer, "Fortitude!" He wonders, "Where do you get that fortitude stuff?" I reply, "Deep down, Terry, deep down."

It's only a game. These are the words used by my family to console me after one of my teams suffers a tough loss (like the seventh game in the 1997 World Series). They usually find me either riding my tractor or laying on the living room floor listening to Nana Mouskouri. I often wonder how much more difficult it must be for the player than for the fan. Fans are protected by distance and a disconnect from the pressures, peaks, and valleys that come with actually playing sports.

It seems to me that batters and pitchers are examples of the most intense and focused instances of individual responsibility. In baseball, it is a conflict between two skilled players that is won most of the time by the pitcher, sometimes by a terrific pitch, sometimes by a less-than-perfect swing. In slow-pitch softball, the spotlight is on the batter; the pitches are pretty much the same. Every player on both teams is watching the batter. The batter's total attention is on the flight of the pitched ball, and the rest of the world stops moving. A hit is joyful—responsibility carried out. An out is disappointing and frustrating—a failed responsibility. Overall, win or lose, playing a sport is an enjoyable experience, largely I believe, because the intensity of individual responsibility in the sporting moment liberates one temporarily from the demands and rigors of life.

Ignominy is grounding into a double play to end the game. We had a long way to go in our last inning, needing eight more runs to tie. I was two for six until my last bat, having grounded out three times. I was determined to meet my responsibility. I focused on that pitched ball as it descended toward me. My swing produced another grounder. Running hard, I was nipped at first for a double play, ending the game. It's not like the winning runs were on base, but my anguish was so visible, the opposing team shortstop came up to me and asked, "Are you okay?" I answered, "Yes, it's only a game."

UMPIRING

The umpires in our league are volunteers. When I was called, I felt an obligation to serve. My wife asked, "Will you get a black-and-white, striped shirt?"

"No, only referees wear those shirts."

"You're refereeing."

"No, I'm umpiring."

"How can umpire be a verb?"

I do get to wear a fluorescent orange vest. The two umpires look like flagmen on a highway construction project.

I am umpiring the games between Teams No. 3 and No. 7. Team No. 3 is the Rosemere Tavern team, wearing their sponsor's gray T-shirts and red hats. There are some serious ballplayers on this team. Eight of them have professional bags holding their personal bats and gear. The bags are hanging on the fence, carefully aligned as if arranged by an interior decorator hired by the team.

Team No. 7 is in blue hats and blue shirts, with "Hamilton-Mylan" and a large number on the back, and in the front over the heart, "Angels" (Hamilton-Mylan is the largest funeral home in Vancouver, Washington). And we are still Team No. 5.

I've been thinking about "No. 5," the name of our team. Softball has a long history of creative and novel names. In organized leagues, uniforms (at least a T-shirt) feature the names of sponsors. Many have been immortalized by championship teams, but most have little impact and probably reflect a favor exercised by a local merchant, saloon, restaurant, or neighborhood business. These names are respectful and proper. In leagues lower on the rung of public awareness and scrutiny (such as intramural competition at colleges), the names flirt with the edges of good taste. A venereal disease clinic in San Francisco fielded a team named "Burning Sensations."[1] My favorite in the intramural league at the University of California at Davis was "3 Balls and You're Weird."[2] An intramural team at Linfield College in Oregon was named the "Masterbatters."

Team names don't have to be long; there have been some good short-word classics. I'll take credit for one. In the early 1970s, I organized a team representing the Department of Obstetrics and Gynecology at the Yale University School of Medicine, composed of faculty and resident doctors, in the Yale fast-pitch league. Our name was the "Nads," and our cheer was, "Go Nads!" I don't know if our name helped, but the Nads won the league championship one year. At the rate No. 5 is going, surely a change won't hurt.

I have never ever umpired. The rulebook that was supposed to be delivered to me never showed up. I figure it can't be that hard. And it isn't. In the first game, I am in the field watching the bases, and in the second game, I am at home plate calling balls and strikes, keeping track of the outs, and trying to keep track of the score (thank goodness, each team has a scorekeeper for today's games). I have only two close calls, runners barely being

beat by throws to first base. All I get are momentary penetrating looks into my eyes by the disgruntled runners. There's no arguing in senior softball!

No angry words, ridicule, or scorn—this is easy. I soon come to the conclusion that all it takes to be a good umpire is a passionate commitment to truth and justice. And for those who need to experience and exert authority, this is a grand opportunity, constrained as it is by time and the dimensions of a ball field. The problem is that no one loves an umpire; it is lonely out there.

"I call 'em as I see 'em." The umpire's motto. It strikes me that this approach is the same as that experienced by a good scientist or a medical clinician, an honest, accurate response to data (the nuts and bolts of knowledge) to the best of one's ability. My goodness, is umpiring a metaphor for living a good life?

GAMES 7 & 8

I'm in the outfield now. When I was younger I enjoyed playing shortstop, feeling like I was in the center of the action. I entered the Air Force at age thirty-one, after five years of specialty training, five years of in-hospital, on-call duty every day and every other night. There was no time for sports during those five years. When I reached Vandenberg Air Force Base, now wearing eyeglasses, I recognized that my reflexes had slowed. I learned that the medical squadron softball team needed a catcher, and I volunteered for the job.

41

Before the season began, Pete and I worked out in the handball courts, not playing handball, but practicing pitching and catching. Pete was a taciturn big man, a forty-five-year-old career Air Force man, an orderly in the hospital, and a wonderful fast-pitch pitcher. We settled on five signals because it quickly became apparent that if I didn't know what was coming, I couldn't catch it. Pete had a fastball, a curve, a change-up, a drop ball, and a riser. The curve and change-up were just for fun. Late in the season in a game when we were far ahead, I told one of the league's best batters that I was going to ask for a change-up. "I want to see what you can do with it," I said, thinking the pressure of the situation would be his undoing. He hit it over the fence. I signaled for the straight fastball when we needed a called strike. The drop ball and especially the riser were for strikeouts.

We had a good team, mostly enlisted men, a few sergeants, and two doctors. We made it through our bracket in the season-ending tournament that first year undefeated. It was the week of the championship game, and *Pete retired!* I would see him in the hospital corridors and say, "Re-up Pete. Please re-up." He would just shake his head. We lost the championship game, 6–2.

Now I am in a more lonesome place, the outfield. I wait for each pitch to deliver me some wanted action, but I recognize that I lack the confidence of my youth when I thought I could catch anything that came near. The secret of slow-pitch softball is that it doesn't matter how good you are; anyone can play and enjoy the game. Nevertheless, I struggle with my competitiveness. I do not like making bad plays. I do not like losing.

Being a Cleveland sports fan, it's not like I haven't had a lot of practice losing. Joe Queenan, on July 20, 2003, wrote in the *New York Times* that "being a sports fan is a matter of processing, analyzing, rationalizing and coping with defeat." I endured forty-one years of losing before the Indians won another American League pennant. One summer, my brother Ted and I went to New York for four *Indians vs. Yankees* games. We lost all four, and after the last loss, we were headed to the hotel on the subway, two Indians fans in their garb surrounded by a packed crowd of loud Yankee fans in their team paraphernalia. I said to my brother, "Anyone can be a Yankee fan. It takes a tough man to be an Indians fan."

I am competitive. I am very competitive. I wouldn't even let my small children win playing HORSE at our driveway basketball hoop. I am also very vocal. My ethnic background (Macedonian) will not permit emotions to be bottled up. I never achieved an athlete's ability to be even-keeled, maintaining a blank facial expression after a game-winning hit or an egregious error. When I hit a ground ball or lose a fly ball in the outfield, I let out an angry yell. When a ball bounces off my mitt in the outfield, I too often fling my beloved baseball glove. Of course, this only attracts more attention to my misplay. I do think my competitiveness has served me well in my academic career, providing good motivation. But I hasten to add that my professional performance reflects a complex mixture of many motivating forces; I am not dominated by my competitiveness.

What is this leading to? It leads to my returning to the batting cages. I was determined to apply my scientific analytic skills to my batting, to make a change if necessary. You have to realize what a major life event this is. I have used the same batting stance since the sixth grade. Omar Vizquel was my favorite Indians player because he used *my* batting stance. Everyone knows you change with aging (some call it maturation). Sure enough, after hitting 250 balls (the first customer of the day gets fifty balls free!), I concluded that I was not getting my body into my swing. I worked out a change: I opened my stance (moving my left foot a few inches away from the plate) and turned my head more toward the pitcher, reasoning that I needed a better look at the ball. I lowered my hands a little and took a bigger step forward with my swing. Looked good and felt good in the batting cage.

Looked so good and felt so good in game conditions, that I was euphoric. In seven at bats I had five strong hits as we lost the first game 15–9 and won the second, 24–10. One of my outs was a pop-up in the infield, but the other was a ball right at the left fielder that almost went over his head. I had six hard-hit drives, and there was no doubt in my mind that my new batting stance allowed me to see the ball better. These games were definitely more fun for me than last week's, and it was so good to end our losing streak. My excitement lasted all night as in a fitful sleep I relived the feel and sound of the bat hitting the ball and the flight of the ball into the outfield. I am off to Brazil next week to lecture, and I already regret having to wait to get back on the diamond in my new batting stance.

Typical Oregon springtime coolness and rain returned this week. Our days have been filled with broken, dark clouds with brief moments of sunshine, but mostly scattered showers that occasionally yielded a deluge of rain. Our ballgames today were threatened with cancellation, but we were fortunate to play on a damp field, experiencing only one short rain shower. Coach Bill's outfit today matched the dark clouds: a black hat, black baseball jersey, black baseball knickers, totally black socks, and black shoes. Not even a single stripe! As the black "tornado" lumbered around the bases and came in to score, he yelled to us on the bench, "I'm faster than I look."

Oren is one of our team's best hitters. He dropped out of high school in Long Beach, California, to pursue his dream of playing baseball. Unable to make a professional team, he enlisted in the Air Force and proceeded to enjoy playing over one hundred games each year all over the world. While in the Air Force, he began and maintained a conversation with a woman through teletype connections. Before ever seeing each other, they decided to marry. After the Air Force, Oren went to work for the Sprint telephone company. He went back to school and obtained his college degree at age forty-three. During his last years with Sprint he was a lobbyist with the state governments in Oregon and Washington, and even at the federal level in Washington, D.C.

Oren and his wife were married for forty-eight years. The last six years were a difficult, painful, and losing struggle with breast cancer. Before his wife passed away, Oren met a woman on a golf course in Arizona who turned out to be an old high-school classmate. She talked him into attending their high school reunion, where Oren and his wife met another classmate, a woman who shared homeroom with Oren for four years and betted with him on baseball games. They became friendly again, and after Oren's wife lost her battle with cancer, true to his style, Oren maintained a letter correspondence with his old classmate, a correspondence that blossomed into love. Next week, Oren is going to the Oregon coast, where, in a ceremony

Oren is one of our team's best hitters. He dropped out of high school in Long Beach, California, to pursue his **dream** of playing baseball.

on the beach, he will marry his old classmate and betting pal. As Oren walked away after our games, I yelled to him, "Have a great honeymoon, but cut it short in time to make our games next week."

Emboldened by my batting success, I returned to the sporting goods store. There were sixty bats (I counted them) on the softball rack. A half hour later, I had three finalists. I alternated swings among the three bats; I hit the metal shelf only once, a whack that resonated throughout the store. The clerks must be used to it because the noise didn't draw anyone, except the man shopping for baseball shoes in the next aisle. I finally decided on a thirty-four-inch, twenty-eight-ounce Worth EST Gold Shell, made of C555 alloy ("containing two times more scandium"). I was a sucker for the sticker that alleged an extra, extra large sweet spot and a "Hyper Flex" whiplash frame that promised ultra-high performance.

Buying a personal bat is a gamble, an expensive gamble. It's like getting married without having lived together. There is no way to know if a good swing in a store aisle will translate into a line drive on the ball field. I quickly realized that choosing a bat was not science. I had to make an emotional judgment based on "feel," a highly personal gut reaction. Now the bat sits highly visible, admired, and pampered in my closet awaiting game conditions.

GAMES
9 & 10; 11 & 12

At a hotel in Brazil, I searched ESPN, CNN, and even EuroSports, and could not find any mention of Team No. 5. I had to wait until my return to learn that we won games 9 & 10 by scores of 21–14 and 18–5. Terry told me that after the games, the team decided that the missing players were the key factor in the victories. This proved to be a prophetic statement as games 11 & 12 were ugly, discouraging losses by scores of 18–9 and 13–5 that even fans, if there were any, would have booed.

Coach Bill attributed last week's good performance to his wearing the color orange. If that's the case, then we don't want to see a repeat of his return to bright red that was featured today.

We have **uniforms.** Well, not exactly; we have **T-shirts.**

Despite the losses, coming back to the team after missing a week was an enjoyable experience. I learned that seventy-seven-year-old Fred played twelve games in the previous four days. How does he do it? Thinking of how my legs feel the day after a game, I asked him if he didn't at least get tired. Fred admitted to feeling a little tired, but only when they play three or more games in one day! Oren didn't get his priorities right and opted for a honeymoon instead of playing in last week's ball games. Of course, his weak hitting this week drew hoots and hollers of "too much honeymoon."

We have uniforms. Well, not exactly; we have T-shirts. The shirts are solid white with small, light-blue lettering on the back (you have to be within ten feet to read it) that proclaims: CB Concrete, Inc. I guess that means we are the "Concretes." And today we played as if we had concrete for gloves and hands. I was no exception. Six balls came to me in the outfield, and I made four errors. One groundball went under my mitt, and three line drives that were catchable with only modest difficulty hit my mitt and dribbled out to land on the ground.

My hitting was fair: three hits in six at bats. I kept fighting an overeagerness that I attributed to my new bat. Good equipment gives confidence, but results are still due to the player's actions, both at bat and in the field. It's like the old saying in fishing when the line breaks and a fish is lost: it's not the line, it's the jerk at the end.

My new T-shirt identifying me as a "Concrete" has my number, 19, in small, two-inch numerals on the left sleeve. There is a pocket on the front over my heart. There are no pockets over the heart on softball uniforms! What in the world is it for, a pen to sign autographs? The shirts come in only one size, extra large. It hangs loosely to my thighs. Finally as I went out to the outfield, Maury said, "Tuck it in. It looks like a dress!" So at the start of the second game, I tucked my shirt in, thinking I might look more like a ball player, and I did catch a fly ball.

The whole team played like concrete. We made error after error, hit weak balls to the infield, and hard-hit balls directly to fielders. I am beginning to like our old name, "Team No. 5," more and more.

Before the game, we debated eyeglasses, another problem unique to older age. I am a strong advocate for "fades," providing a seamless transition from distant to near vision. Others prefer traditional bifocals, finding it hard to adjust to fades. Big Fred in right field plays with sunglasses that are not his usual bifocals. He guesses where the ball will be in the last ten feet before it reaches him. Makes you wonder how many misplayed balls are because of the wrong eyeglasses?

These games were the first time that I didn't feel upbeat and even exhilarated afterward. Intellectually, I understand that I shouldn't expect old skills to come back after so many years of not playing softball. The problem is that the emotions are the same as when I was younger. I have a hard time tolerating a poor performance, and a sense of despair lingered for several days after these games. Just like I had previously relived my good at bats with solid hits, I kept picturing my mitt reaching out, the ball hitting the pocket, and a sad, pathetic drop of the ball to the ground. As one player said to me, "After all, we are all legends in our own minds!"

This is obviously something that will require an adjustment, because the odds are that poor performance at my age will not be an isolated or rare occurrence. I will have to call on the mellow wisdom that is supposed to accumulate with aging, if only I can find where it is stored, available for use.

Bill is our coach for a reason. His advice was an old athletic cliché that never loses its meaning or its relevance. "Let it go. It's over. Look forward to the next game."

GAMES 13 & 14

Sporadic raindrops were hitting my windshield as I set out for our games. By the time I was halfway there it was raining hard. It made me remember one of the most dramatic Cleveland Browns games I ever saw.

A serious thunderstorm suddenly surrounded old Cleveland Stadium during the second half of the Browns game. The thunder, darkness, and driving rain seemed to be focused and intensified within the confines of the steel and concrete oval. About twenty-five young men in the end-zone bleachers embraced the storm. Stripped to their bare chests, they began to yell, sing, and dance. Their spirit infected the crowd. Soon progressively louder cheering followed every thunderclap, the crowd dueling with the lightning. The Browns responded to the crowd's enthusiasm, and the defense stiffened. A punt forced the Browns offense to start near its own goal line. During a television time out, the wind and rain stopped, the clouds parted, and the sun began to shine on the field, a seemingly miraculous change that inspired the fans to a new height of excitement and cheering. Responding to the crowd, the Browns drove the length of the field to pull ahead in the last thirty-eight seconds of the game.

I found five of my teammates already at the ball field. Within a half an hour the rain stopped, and we played our games under dark and threatening clouds, with only an occasional light sprinkle of rain. Remarkably, not a single player for either team failed to show up for the games.

We lost again, by scores of 12–5 and 15–7 (five of the seven runs coming in one inning). By now, we are following an established pattern, providing the opposing team with multiple opportunities because of fielding errors. Despite our losses, the games were a little more satisfying for me as I fielded six chances in the outfield with no errors. Little Fred in left field made the defensive play of the game, running in and snaring a drive at his shoe tops just before it hit the ground. I told him that I didn't think he could bend over so far. He said, "Surprised me too."

Our hitting also followed a familiar pattern: line drives, fly balls, and grounders hit directly to fielders. We had too many "no piss" innings, meaning that we rapidly made three outs, leaving guys to complain there was no time to use the honey bucket.

I was surprised when I first came up to bat to hear the opposing pitcher turn to his fielders and say, "good hitter." I promptly hit what may have been my hardest smash of the season thus far—on a clothesline directly to the third baseman. I went two for six; my two hits were grounders past the infield. My other hard-hit ball went right to the left fielder. On one at bat I was served four unhittable balls for a walk. As I went to first base, I had to agree with Terry, who drew a walk and said, "I didn't drive this far to just walk." Frank, our excellent infielder, drives 120 miles round trip to play in our games. He has a great license plate. It reads, "5 for 5."

Our team is obviously not a powerhouse in the league. We are legitimate underdogs in every game. But fans love underdogs, because victory is so much sweeter when an underdog wins. I have noticed the same older woman sitting on a lawn chair behind home plate at each of our games. I went up to her and said, "You are our best fan. In fact, usually you are our only fan." She said, "I have the nitro in my purse!"

...fans love **underdogs,** because victory is so much **sweeter** when an underdog wins.

I'll miss next week's games; it is the week of my annual fly-fishing trip on the Deschutes River. When I notified Coach Bill that I wouldn't be there for the games, Terry let me have it. "My understanding is that this is total body commitment, no vacations, get here early for the games, use your spare time in the batting cage." Despite knowing that he was being playful, I was surprised when I realized he had managed to stir up some guilt in me. Then I thought if he knew how much time I spent thinking about our games, pounding a ball into my mitt, grieving over our losses, and suffering through mental replays of my errors and poor at bats, I am confident he would spare me the guilt. Well...maybe not.

GAMES
15 & 16; 17 & 18

We are no longer the "Concretes." The white shirts were leftovers from last year that we were using temporarily awaiting new shirts from our sponsor. Our new fluorescent green T-shirts can be seen from a long distance. There are no numbers on the shirts, and I was happy to see that there are no pockets in the front over our hearts. The front proclaims our sponsor in small black letters:

OXFORD
ATHLETIC CLUB

Standing in the outfield
and looking at the
bright green,
blank backs
of our shirts...

...we look like
lime popsicles
scattered about
the field.

Above the name of our sponsor, directly in the center, sits a large, black "O," measuring 6.5 x 6.5 inches. I have declared us to be the "Os," and not the "Zeros." Standing in the outfield and looking at the bright green, blank backs of our shirts, we look like lime popsicles scattered about the field.

This was the week after the Oregon State University baseball team won the national championship. Coach Bill is a rabid Beavers fan, and he proudly wore his orange hat and orange knee-length socks that combined with our new T-shirts to produce a jarring impact on the eyes.

It was a great evening for softball! There was a gentle breeze, and the temperature was pleasantly warm. It was perfect for shorts, revealing some interesting sights. Don won the prize for his startlingly white, smooth legs that looked like marble columns from a Greek

Don

Don is still working **full time** as a computer programmer, forcing him to endure a **ninety-minute** drive in rush-hour traffic to make our games. He says that he will retire as soon as he and his wife are eligible for **Medicare.**

temple. Don no longer wears his favorite "Aches and Pains" shirt. He is still working full time as a computer programmer, forcing him to endure a ninety-minute drive in rush-hour traffic to make our games. He says that he will retire as soon as he and his wife are eligible for Medicare.

Our team split the games last week, losing the first one 19–8, and coming from behind to win the second. It was the last inning of the second game, and we were down four runs, 19–15. No one made an out, and five consecutive hits later, we won 20–19. Maury tripled to bring us within one run of tying the game. Little Fred, our left fielder, hit a walk-off home run to record a thrilling, rare victory for us, and I wish I had been there to pound on Fred. He is one of our best players at bat and in the field. Fred grew up in California and played basketball for Stanford. In Oregon, he worked for the aluminum company until he retired, and he has played softball for the last thirty years.

This week we returned to our losing ways, dropping two by scores of 18–8 and 11–8, in front of a real crowd. There must have been ten relatives sitting on the grass. I was happy to have no errors in the field, but my hitting was a little frustrating, two for five with too many ground balls. I decided my new bat was just a little top heavy. I needed to find the proper balance point.

Little Fred

After experimenting at the batting cage, I enlarged the knob at the end of the bat by winding layers of black electrician's tape at the bottom of the handle. I could have simply "choked up," moving my hands up the handle each time. But true to my compulsive nature, I wanted my hands to be guided to the same exact location each time I gripped the bat. But I still hit too many ground balls.

I learned that Big Fred, our ex-school teacher and right fielder, has long been known by a nickname, "The Indian." He said a team consisting mainly of Italians gave it to him. I wondered why they chose that name, and Fred gave me a clear explanation, "They couldn't tell a German from an Indian."

Big Fred

It struck me that a senior men's softball team is an example of Darwinian selection. These guys have been active in sports all their lives. Those who become frustrated by schedule requirements, drive long distances for games, and are too often recovering from pulled and stiff muscles tend to give up. Others have bodies that for one reason or another no longer permit demanding physical exercise. The players on this field have endured and continue to survive the mental and physical challenges of playing ball. I am pleased and fortunate to be included in their company.

Terry likes to say (repeatedly) that "sports are humblelizing." As soon as you have done something good, you turn around and do something bad. We see it in major league baseball players who to a man cannot escape the experience of a slump, whether it is batting or pitching. We see a top-notch sports team lose a game on a physical or mental mistake,

GAMES
19 & 20

The "Lime Popsicles" took the field and proceeded to lose two more games. However, the games were hard fought with the lead swinging back and forth until our opponent snatched victory from the jaws of defeat in the last inning of each game, by scores of 11–8 and 18–17. Halfway through our second game we were ahead 10–4. We lost and regained the lead in the last inning 17–15 only to succumb to a three-run walk-off home run that soared over our outfielder's heads in left-center field.

I made a hard, painful (and costly) decision. I divorced my bat. A good friend of mine once said, "The philosophy of America is written in country music." I think "wrong bat" should be added to the country song litany of failed loves, railroad accidents, lost dogs, and old trucks.

When I purchased the bat, I was totally aware of the importance of bat weight and that lighter bats produce greater bat speed, the most important ingredient in the mix of factors that leads to a good hit. Yet I bought a twenty-eight-ounce bat, reasoning that I was strong enough to swing it, and that a touch of extra weight would allow me to wait on the pitched ball, another important factor in hitting a slowly pitched softball. So much for my strength! Disappointed in too many ground balls, I experimented with the other available bats and found that I do better with a twenty-six-ounce bat. But I had a problem. I hesitated to reveal my bad judgment to my wife by buying another bat this season. So I reminded her of something from T. Boone Pickens that I am fond of quoting, "At my age, a dollar saved is a dollar wasted."

Batting with my new thirty-four-inch, twenty-six-ounce, dark red Easton "Havoc," I had two line drives in the first game directly to the third baseman and shortstop. In the second game, I had two good hits, the second a great drive flying far over the left fielder.

In the second game, I had two good hits, the second a great drive **flying far** over the left fielder.

Tim and Coach Bill

Blood **cascading** down his face from lacerations on his forehead and below his nose, he looked like a true **warrior...**

Experiencing these repeated losses is getting me down. It is often said that losing builds character, but at our age, further character building is not needed. The moral victory of still being healthy and alive only goes so far. Endless philosophizing gets tiresome. I am very vocal in the field and on the bench, congratulating teammates on good plays and exhorting teammates in the batter's box. But suddenly I became aware that the losing was making me quiet. Coach Bill has thanked me for my enthusiasm, and so I resolved once again, "It's only a game," and I vowed to keep up my energy and spirits.

It was not difficult to be involved and energetic in these two games. Both games were close battles with good defense (by both teams for a change). In the last two innings of the second game we began to take casualties. Coach Bill was halfway to first base when he tore a muscle in his left thigh. His leg gave out and he collapsed to the ground with his body straight out pointing at first base, like one of Oregon's old growth Douglas fir trees being cut down. He fell so quickly and so hard, he had no time to protect his body with his hands. His face hit the ground, plowing a furrow with his nose and filling his mouth with dirt.

I rushed to his side with one concern in my mind, to make sure he had no chest pain and breathing was not a problem. When he rolled over, blood cascading down his face from lacerations on his forehead and below his nose, he looked like a true warrior. His teammates insisted on taking a picture. Coach Bill was mainly worried over his wife's reaction, "She's going to kill me." I called later that night and learned that she had taken good care of him and had already tucked him into bed.

In the very next inning, Terry at shortstop dropped to the ground after reaching for a ground ball, holding his left hamstring. Long minutes followed as Terry tried to stand and could not, then tried to walk and could not. But gradually he regained mobility and stayed in the game.

After each injury, the very small crowd watching our games was noticeably hushed. Our sparse crowds remind me of many years of Cleveland Indians baseball when only a few thousand fans attended the games in the old stadium.

Terry

My brother and I are in a movie, the cult film *Major League.* Most Indians fans have viewed this movie many times because for years it was the only winning season we could experience. One night after an Indians game, they filmed a crowd scene. Not many of us were there so they brought us all into a crowd behind the first base line. A camera went back and forth as we repeatedly stood and cheered. We probably hit the cutting floor because I have never spied us in the movie, and I know that most, if not all of the baseball scenes, were filmed in the old Milwaukee ball park. But I like to think we are immortalized in that movie, a favorite with thousands of Indians fans.

GAMES 21 & 22

We immediately fell behind 3 to 0 in the first inning and I thought, here we go again. But no, this was our night. We won the first game 18–7 and the second, 19–11, with timely hitting and good defense. In the first game we had three 1-2-3 defensive innings in a row.

I was four for seven in the two games, three for four in the first game, and one hit, a walk, a fly ball, and on base on an error in the second game. But best of all, I made my best catch of the season thus far in the second inning of the second game.

It was a hard line drive over the second baseman's head. I got a good jump on the ball, running to my left. With my mitt reaching straight out, I dove for the ball, caught it, hit the ground hard on my left shoulder, rolled to my feet, and threw to my relay man. It is tough to find words to describe how good it felt to make that catch. I soaked up the congratulations of my teammates (even two players from the other team went out of their way to high five me at the end of the inning). Maury said, "Are you okay? How's your shoulder?" I told him, "If there is a bruise on my shoulder, I am going to love showing it to people."

Tim said, "I have the catch digitized. It will be on ESPN Sportscenter." "I'm willing to stay up late for that," I said. Tim pointed out, "You'll have to. It's only going to be on the 3 AM show."

Coach Bill and Terry still cannot run after their injuries almost two weeks ago. But they came to the game, rooting us on, and coaching at first base and third base. Bill's face lacerations healed nicely, but he developed a huge hematoma at the site of his muscle tear in his left thigh. Terry had trouble walking for days after his hamstring injury.

After the first inning of the first game, we were leading throughout the rest of the night, the cause of the most upbeat and exhilarating mood we have had all season. There was a constant flow of jokes, teases, and gibes. When Big Fred reached second base after a good hit, he was rewarded by cheers from the bench, "Triple into a double, triple into a double." "Way to go, Iron Glove" greeted our center fielder after he dropped a fly ball.

After my great catch, I was walking in from the outfield at the end of an inning, and

Terry yelled, "Look at everyone. They are all walking, because of you. Run off the field. You make a great catch, you have to be a leader."

"Wow, Terry, are you telling me I have to be a role model?"

"That's right, you have to set a good example."

"Damn!"

"And that's another thing. Watch your mouth."

"Darn!"

"That's better."

I was thrown out at first base on a groundball, and as I jogged off the field, I said to Terry, "If I had better coaching, I would have been safe." He replied, "You're right. I'm assuming too much!"

Maury, our seventy-eight-year-old third baseman, continues to amaze me. With quick reflexes he snatches line drives going over his head or to his side. He snares hard-hit ground balls and easily makes an accurate long throw to first base. And he is one of our best hitters. I'm thinking that 45 SPF stuff he slathers on must have something else in it. After all, there is no urine testing in senior softball—it would take too long to collect a sample.

Maury, our seventy-eight-year-old third baseman, continues to **amaze** me.

Maury

Last weekend, Maury and Big Fred went to Reno to play softball. Each night they went out on the town. Well, they didn't go far—to Mel's Diner in the Sands Hotel. Maury had the large size hot fudge sundae and Fred a root-beer float. And they did the same thing three nights in a row. They loved telling us about it.

I was in Connecticut last week for my daughter Jane's wedding. I told her that I had dreamed of contacting Frank Deford with the hope of having an excerpt of this softball journal published in *Sports Illustrated*. We enjoy listening to Deford on National Public Radio, and I knew that Deford lived in Connecticut. My daughter said, "Let's check the phone book." Sure enough there was Deford's address, and my daughter instantly recognized that it was not far from her home in Trumbull. She said, "Let's go over, ring his doorbell, and deliver the journal." "You're kidding," I said, "I can't do anything that brazen." My wife joined the discussion, and by the end of the afternoon, they had talked me into it.

With excitement, we hatched a plan to print out the journal, drive over the next morning to Deford's house, and if it looked inviting and not forbidding (like surrounded by a moat and closed gate), I would ring the doorbell and hand deliver what I have written thus far. First, I had to endure a long, restless night rehearsing what I would say. My anxiety increased progressively and by the time we drove past the house, I was downright scared.

The house sat close to the road with an inviting driveway, and in the open garage we spied an automobile with its lights on, someone just arriving or leaving. My daughter turned the car around and asked, "Do you have the nerve to walk up the driveway?" And before I could answer, she pulled in the drive. "Okay," I said, "here I go." With zero confidence and great trepidation, I walked weak-kneed to the garage.

Before I reached the inside doorway, Mrs. Deford, having watched me walk up the drive, emerged with an appropriately stern look, stood at the top of the steps looking tall and imposing, and asked, "Can I help you?" I said, "Forgive me for walking up your driveway. I'm from Portland, Oregon, visiting Connecticut for my daughter's wedding. I'm seventy-one years old and just started playing softball again. I'm writing a journal and I wanted to give it to Mr. Deford."

She smiled. *She smiled!* The smile melted my anxiety. She said, "He's traveling, but I would be happy to give it to him." I told her, "I was so scared walking up your driveway. Thank you so much for your smile." We parted with happy thoughts about the upcoming wedding.

When I got in the car and we drove away, I was so relieved. I reached over and gave my daughter a big hug and told her that I never would have done such a brash thing without her help and encouragement. We swerved just a little, and fortunately the green mailbox by the curb remained standing and untouched.

I told the story to the guys, and now they want to know when they will be in *Sports Illustrated.*

GAMES 23 & 24

It was a tense and exciting moment on a beautiful evening of good softball. The chatter on our bench was loud and upbeat. We were up for our last at bat, trailing 12–11. It was a back and forth game, with hard hitting and sharp defense. My third hit put men at second and third, and Norm hit a sharp line drive single to the outfield, driving in the game-winning run, 13–12. We were so energized, we sprinted to a 12–0 lead in the second game, ultimately winning 12–5. We have a winning streak!

Norm

Maury continued to set a blistering pace, stroking deep line drives with his bat and gloving any ball that came near him. What a great ballplayer he must have been in his younger days. Incredibly, he took a year off two years ago to have a total hip replacement. With or without an artificial hip, he certainly is the best seventy-eight-year-old ballplayer I have ever seen. Each time Maury bats, it's like a scene from *The Natural* with Roy Hobbs and his favorite bat, "Wonderboy." Maury removes his black bat from his equipment bag hanging on the fence only when it is his turn to bat. After batting, he carefully returns the bat to his bag, first inserting the bat into its very own, soft, knitted, white sock. This bat is going to last a long time.

I have a personal streak going of errorless play in the outfield: two fly balls and several well-played grounders in today's games. Well, there was the misjudged fly ball coming straight at me that went over my head. But mental errors don't show up in the scorebook!

Maury

Terry noticed something on the baseball shoe of the opposing pitcher and asked me what it was.

"I don't know. Is it a metal plate covering the toe?"
"No, it's duct tape!"
"You can get it for $1.50 at Home Depot, but it costs $15 at the sporting goods store."

Terry showed me his silver bat, the first aluminum bat he ever purchased. It cost $9.99. Although it was supposed to weigh twenty-six ounces, it had a very light feel to its swing. Terry decided to make it heavier. He drilled a small hole in the handle end of the bat, and filled the end of the bat with water. But when he took his batting stance, the water shifted into the handle and leaked on him. He bought a second bat for $19.99.

Tim is our main pitcher, but he can play anywhere, in the infield or in the outfield as the rover, the outfielder who tries to outguess the hitter by being stationed in the very spot the ball will be hit. Tim is not a large man, but he has a compact athletic body on a pair of thick football legs that are so buff he frequently requests a courtesy runner to avoid pulling a muscle. He carries himself with military bearing, something that is not surprising considering his long and distinguished military career. After graduating from the U. S. Naval Academy where he played center and middle linebacker, Tim participated in three deployments during the Vietnam War. He has commanded air squadrons on aircraft carriers, served as the Operations Officer and Executive Officer of the *USS Ranger*, and commanded the *USS Ogden* that participated in the Valdez oil spill cleanup. During Operation Desert Storm, Tim commanded the *USS Peleliu*, the flagship for the Eleventh Marine Expeditionary Unit. Tim retired in 1994 after thirty years of active duty and directed a Naval ROTC high school unit in Zion, Illinois. He was named to Who's Who of American Teachers and coached baseball, football, and wrestling, and at the same time

Tim

he was in charge of the Midwest Leadership Academy, a two-week summer experience for high-school military cadets. He is currently serving as executive director of the *USS Ranger* Museum Foundation, an organization dedicated to saving and preserving the *USS Ranger*.

Considering his experiences and leadership roles, it is amazing that Tim doesn't come close to the stereotypical image of a hard-driving, commanding military chief. Perhaps that is one of the secrets of his success; he is personable, easygoing, with a ready smile that lights up his mustachioed face. I told him he didn't resemble any of the commanders I encountered in the Air Force. He said, "I'm a pilot. We're into bravado, not the rest of that stuff." Our teammates sometimes affectionately call Tim "Captain Tailhook." We also call him "Admiral" after a good hit and "Ensign" when he makes an out.

The tenderness and bruise on the top of my left shoulder took several days to heal, a pleasant process because it repeatedly stimulated me to relive and enjoy my wonderful catch. Coach Bill and Terry are still hobbled by their muscle injuries, but they insisted on playing. Bill grimaced with each fielding play at first base, then limped around in a circle until he recovered. We were rewarded for their persistence by some good hitting. Bill had a massive drive over the left fielder's head. He keeps careful track of his hits; I think he calculates his batting average after each game.

Coach Bill

He keeps **careful** track of his hits; I think he calculates his **batting** **average** after each game.

Coach Bill noted the attention I was giving to his leg attire. He carefully explained to me that when playing first base, the shortstop and third baseman throw from the sun into shadows, and his legs give them a discernable target. He remembers vividly an inning he sat out last year when the shortstop threw the ball at the coach whose legs were likewise covered with long socks. Coach Bill is convinced his high socks help the infielders, "That's my reason, and I am sticking to it."

I have noticed that just like younger sportspeople, older slow-pitch softball players do not allow aches and pains or minor injuries and illnesses to prevent their showing up for the ball games. My serious problem is a "trigger finger" or to be more precise, a trigger thumb. The flexing of the distal joints of the fingers requires a tendon attached to a muscle in the hand to travel to the finger bones through a capsular sheath, like a train passing through a tunnel. Inflammation of this tendon from trauma or repetitive motion produces an enlargement that makes it difficult, if not impossible, for the tendon to move through the tunnel. My trigger thumb followed the operation of a gasoline-powered hedge trimmer over an hour's time.

I had no idea what was wrong with my thumb. What would a gynecologist know about fingers? Okay, don't answer that one. I kept thinking it would get better, but after eight weeks, I decided it was time to see an orthopedic surgeon, one who specializes in the hand. It was a two-second diagnosis by the orthopod, a large, athletic man of seemingly great strength.

> "You have a trigger finger. But no problem, it is easily fixed with surgery."
> "Wait, I can't have surgery. I'm playing softball."
> "Well, we could first try injecting the joint with cortisone. It may not get better, but there is chance that it would, and if it returns, we can operate later."
> "What's the down side?"
> "The injection hurts."
> "Who is going to hold me down?"
> "Don't worry, I'll hold you down."

Yikes! He was right. It really hurt. I laid down, and the orthopod firmly grasped my left hand in his left hand that was obviously and thankfully much larger. He inserted the needle into the joint at the base of my thumb and injected the cortisone, as my right leg rose straight into the air.

"I think I got it in."
"It sure felt like it."

It was obvious to me that my decision-making revolved around playing softball. Taking a chance on the cortisone and postponing surgery was the only option. I did not want to miss any games. I did not want to tell my teammates that I couldn't play because of a trigger finger.

To my great surprise and delight, I received a letter from Frank Deford only five days after walking up his driveway. He enjoyed the journal and provided the name of an editor at *Sports Illustrated*. Even if *Sports Illustrated* has no interest in the journal, the story adds to the fun of this summer of softball.

GAMES 25 & 26

We are becoming a powerhouse. Playing the team with the best record in our league, we walloped them in the first game, 23–0, and won the second game, 8–2. I was zero for three in the first game, but to say I was not needed is a massive understatement. We could barely believe what we were seeing as our guys hit drive after drive into the outfield, home runs way over the outfielder's heads.

Terry was a **web gem** at second base.

It wasn't just great hitting. A shutout in the first game! Shutouts are unheard of in slow-pitch softball! We made all the routine defensive plays and many spectacular ones. If we made an error, I can't remember it. Terry was a web gem at second base. One rapid-fire double play began with Terry falling to his right, snaring a hard-hit ground ball, and flipping it to second. Later, he told me that he fell because he stepped on his foot, his glove happened to hit the ball, and with dirt in his eyes he got mixed up and thought he was throwing to first base!

I caught five fly balls in the outfield with only one adventure. A very high fly was falling between me and Big Fred in right field. I ran back, reached up, and the ball smacked me on the inside of my left forearm, caromed off to my chest, and bounced up so that I could cradle it with both arms. Laughing, I threw the ball into second base, and ever since I have been admiring the perfectly round bruise on my forearm.

Maury injured his hamstring in last week's game and aggravated it this past weekend. When I was told he wouldn't be coming to today's games, I was surprised by my reaction. Here is a man I only know as a teammate, and I realized that I was saddened by his absence; I missed him. Maury showed up halfway through the second game to sit on a lawn chair and cheer us on. I was really happy to see him. Anyone who has played a team sport knows that the fun of participation is more than the actual playing. It is special to be a teammate, giving and receiving encouraging support, warm banter, smile-provoking joking and gibing, the sharing of winning and especially defeats. I was three for three in the second game, and after my third hit, Maury said, "Way to go, Slugger." I love that Maury.

We have more casualties. Oren and Bill are so limited by painful, bad knees that they have retired for the season. I am sure this was not an easy decision. I have watched them walking with a gimp, running the bases slowly and tenderly, grimacing when they flex, turn, and twist. Many times, someone is heard to say, "As long as it's fun, you keep going." Every one of us still playing is even more grateful to be still out there when someone gives it up.

Frank, our great infielder and hitter (old "5 for 5"), played in a tournament over the weekend and witnessed a one-of-a-kind happening. A teammate hit a triple, and in his excitement, he rapidly ran the bases never dropping his bat. There he stood on third base, still holding his bat, and wondering, "Why am I still holding my bat?" The game was held up as the umpires went to the rule book to learn that he was entitled to remain at third. The bat had to go.

Frank & Tim

Today was Tim's birthday. We didn't sing for him, but listened appreciatively as he told us his birthday story. He attended a luncheon today for Naval Academy alumni. Thinking he would present everyone with a surprise desert, he bought his own birthday cake and secreted it into the kitchen. However, by the time the moderator remembered the cake, it was too late. The waiters ate the cake.

Going into today's games, here are the league standings:

Team No. 1	16 wins	8 losses
Team No. 7	15	6
Team No. 8	15	6
Team No. 4	14	12
Team No. 6	12	10
Team No. 5	9	15
Team No. 3	8	18
Team No. 2	6	20

I fear that our surge into excellence will bring high expectations. Coach Bill is already talking of going unbeaten the rest of the year to miraculously gain a winning record.

THE TWO-PITCH TOURNAMENT

Six of the eight teams in our league gathered on a pleasant Saturday morning to spend a day with softball at a city park. Players from the other two teams were distributed to make up for players who could not be there. The park had three well-manicured softball fields with small bleachers and outfield fences. Taking about an hour to play a game, each team played four of the other teams. When a team was batting, each batter faced a pitcher from his own team (to ensure good pitches), and only two pitches were allowed.

There is no time to waste. You swing at any pitched ball that can be reached by a bat. At the end of four games, the team with the best combination of wins and total runs scored is declared the winner.

We were missing five of our regular players, including three of our best hitters and fielders: Maury (still healing his pulled muscle), "5 for 5" Frank, and Little Fred, our left fielder. Nevertheless we had a great first game, going ahead by a score of 18–14 in the top of the last inning, and holding on to win 18–17. I had a nice line drive to knock in the fifth run in an inning, but the rest of my at bats were an indication of a disappointing batting day to come. I remembered Frank's story of the ballplayer standing on third base holding his bat, when disgruntled over yet another ground ball for an out, I was trotting out to the outfield, and I reached second base before I realized I didn't have my mitt. I was still holding my bat!

Everyone's energy progressively waned with each succeeding game. Strong hits became increasingly few and far between. Tied in the last inning of the second game, we lost 7–6 when a fly ball that could have been the third out skipped under an outfielder's glove. We lost the next two games, 11–3 and 8–4. For the entire day, I had only two hits in fifteen at bats. Batting second in the lineup for the first game, I was appropriately demoted to eighth in the last game.

One of my at bats was the epitome of my day. As I prepared myself in the batter's box, I could hear Terry yelling for all to hear, "Don't be anxious. Get set. Weight on your back foot. Stride forward with power. Go get 'em." I concentrated on keeping my eyes glued to the ball. Striding forward with a compact, smooth swing, I smote that ball. Unfortunately, I just nicked the ball on the end of the bat. It popped up about eight feet in the air, hitting the ground no more than fifteen feet toward third base—a spinner. Amazingly, when the ball hit the ground, it just sat there, spinning round and round like it was trying to burrow into the earth to hide its shame. By the time it was fielded, I was at first base. I couldn't fault the ball; I was too embarrassed to call it a hit.

At least it was a different story in the field. Another errorless day! Coach Bill said he was impressed, and I was not surprised to learn that he knew exactly how many fly balls I have caught without an error. At any time, he can give you an instant up-to-date calculation of his batting average. He calls himself a "statmaster," and I call him a "walking spreadsheet."

> Amazingly, when the ball hit the ground, it just sat there, spinning **round and round** like it was trying to burrow into the earth to hide its shame.

I was coming in from the outfield and I detoured over to the two older women sitting on lawn chairs in the shade behind the fence along the left field line. I said, "Come on ladies; we need some cheering." They answered, "We are cheering. You guys are hard of hearing."

After the games, seventy-five ballplayers came together with their families for a picnic. I learned why everyone knew each other well. Every year a new mix of players is assigned to each team, trying to equalize the competitive ability of each team. But equally important, over time this allows the players to get to know most of the men in the league. It's a great philosophy, adding to the warm fellowship that extends throughout the league. That friendship was very noticeable at the picnic, with players and families enjoying each other. My initial reaction to the two-pitch tournament followed by a picnic was lukewarm at best. I walked away that afternoon feeling really good, uplifted by the close companionship, and next year, this will be a high priority day that I will be sure not to miss.

The news of my journal is slowly spreading. After an entertaining incident or a particularly piquant comment, a player will catch my eye and say, "Write that down!"

GAMES 27 & 28

Eight games in a row! We continued to hit with power and to dazzle ourselves with our defense. We won the first game 17–11. The ball was flying so high and far that Tim, our pitcher, said, "This game ball seems livelier than usual." Norm explained that it was because of global warming.

Tim hit a home run over the right-field fence in the first game, and then he did it again in the second game. I can only dream of something like that. In fact,

91

Larry

my hitting continues to be exasperating. I was one for three in each game, plus a sacrifice fly on a deep fly ball to the left fielder. My teammates have diagnosed my problem. They claim that I am striding into the ball too late, thus hitting the ball with my weight on my back foot. It's back to the batting cage for me to test that diagnosis.

Our defense has been remarkable. No dropped balls in the outfield and accurate throws to the right base after a hit as the infielders make loud and correct calls to us. The infield is racking up multiple double plays. Terry is making play after play at second base. He attributes it to his glove that he calls "Kirby" after the vacuum cleaner company. He also says that it is important to talk to your mitt. I told him that is difficult when your mitt is made in Japan.

Larry joined our team midway through the season, and he is one of the major factors in our improved performance since then. He played fast-pitch softball at third base most of his life. His job as purchasing agent for Crown-Zellerbach took him to many cities. Wherever he was, he either joined a team or formed a team and played in a league. Larry is one of our best hitters, and without question, he is the fastest runner on our team. His speed on the bases has accounted for many runs, and hardly a ball gets by him in center field. He also makes a major contribution with his enthusiasm and constant chatter.

We were ahead by four runs in the sixth inning of the second game and trying to stop a rally by our opponents. Two men were on base when the batter drove one to my left and over my head. I ran six steps to my left and back, leaped into the air, reached up with an extended arm, and caught the ball in the webbing of my mitt. It was such a coordinated moment and so smooth that I never stumbled. I have to admit I was startled to see the ball in my glove, but I managed to hide that reaction as I cooly turned and threw the ball into the infield.

Frank & Big Fred

The fun of a great catch comes afterward, coming off the field to the reception of your teammates. High fives, slaps on the back, laughing and yelling—the moment instantly enters your mental registry of great plays in your life, none ever forgotten. Maury, holding a ball and pen, asked for my autograph. He got a hug instead. Of course, I had to endure some friendly sarcastic reactions to my leaping ability. Frank said I was so high that he thought he could slip the Hood River Yellow Pages under me. We won the second game 14–8.

GAMES 29 & 30

We began our first game lacking the confidence that should have been inspired by an eight-game winning streak because we were missing three of our best fielders and hitters, and one of the three was our best pitcher. But we were all happy to see Maury back on the ball field. Players drawn from the taxi squad replaced our missing teammates.

The original taxi squad can be traced to one of my favorite teams, the Cleveland Browns. The first owner of the Browns,

Maury

Mickey McBride, also owned a taxi service in Cleveland. When Paul Brown cut from the team players that he wanted to hold in reserve, McBride gave them jobs as cab drivers; hence, the "taxi squad." Just like the taxi cab drivers, the talent of our replacements didn't match the skills of our missing players. We were soundly beaten in the first game 16–7.

In the first inning, I ran after a drive to my right, reached up and across my body with my mitt, snared the ball, and tumbled over, coming to my feet to throw the ball in to the infield. I punched the air with my fist, but I should have remembered that "sports are *humblelizing*." An inning later, I drifted back for a fly ball to my left that I had lined up all the way. As the ball hit my glove, inexplicably I closed my mitt prematurely and the ball bounced away. My errorless streak was over. This was followed two innings later by a drive over second base. I was certain I was going to catch it in front of me, but by the time I took two steps in, it was obvious the ball was going over my head. I backpedaled and extended my arms up as high as I could. Maury said later that when he saw my arms go up, he was sure I was going to make another spectacular catch. The only thing spectacular was my awkward fall to the ground as my feet got in my way.

We showed some grit, and to our credit, we didn't roll over in the second game. In the top half of the last inning, the score was tied 15–15. We had two men on base, and seventy-seven-year-old Big Fred came up to bat. I am five-feet, eight-inches tall and weigh 150 pounds. Almost all of my teammates are taller than I am and outweigh me by thirty to fifty pounds. It is obvious why he is "Big Fred" when I stand next to him.

Left-hand-hitting Fred hit the first pitch, and the ball soared over the right field fence for a three-run home run. We mobbed him at the plate. Fred asked, "Did it go over the fence?" I said, "Yes, didn't you see it?" He answered, "No, I can't see that far." In the last half of the inning, we held them to one run, and won 18–16.

Big Fred

It is **obvious** why he is **"Big Fred"** when I stand next to him.

I visited the batting cage once again to battle my batting slump, and I'm not sure if it helped. I was one for two, plus a walk in each game. But I made up for my error and misjudged ball in the first game with another great catch in the second game. This time

Norm

it was a line drive over second base that was going to fall in for a base hit. I ran forward, dove straight ahead, and snagged the ball in my webbing right off the grass. I slid forward accumulating beautiful grass stains. I bounced to my feet, laughing with pleasure.

Norm was hitting the ball well, driving in some critical runs. In fact, we had a five-run inning in which every key hit came from the bottom of our batting order. Running from first base, around second, and heading to third, Norm pulled his right hamstring muscle. He painfully limped off the field, and then went home. Only in senior softball is it acceptable to go home after an injury.

Because of our missing players, we had an overabundance of players who required courtesy runners. These were very physically demanding games for me. Besides repeatedly throwing my body on the outfield ground, I was running for someone practically every inning. Coach Bill, still a bit gimpy, was getting on base and accepting a courtesy runner each time. After a drive to left field, the only teammate available to run for Bill was Maury, our seventy-eight-year-old third basemen. Bill came off the field and said to me, "That's embarrassing. My runner is the oldest man on the team, and this is his first game back from an injured leg."

Our record is now fourteen wins and sixteen losses. Coach Bill made sure everyone is aware that we can avoid a losing season by taking two next week.

Coach Bill

GAMES 31 & 32

From rookie to manager in one season! Coach Bill and Terry are ardent Oregon State University fans. Without equivocating, they chose to attend the Beaver's opening football game instead of playing softball. Coach Bill asked me to be the designated manager for the last games of the season. I was honored and flattered, thinking I was being rewarded for my enthusiasm and the fact that I arrived very early for every game (I tell my family that it is a harmless obsession). Then I learned that my major responsibility was to collect our lime-green T-shirts and wash them. Even then, I accepted Coach Bill's request with pleasure and a feeling of gratitude.

We did it! We won two tightly contested games to end the season with sixteen wins and sixteen losses, going thirteen and one in our last fourteen games. I was one for three in each game, but my four outs were all well-hit balls. They were so well hit that each one required a spectacular defensive play to rob me of a hit. In the second to the last inning in the first game, we scored five to move ahead 15–12. We held them to one run in the last inning and won 15–13. The second game was also a tense affair. Entering the last inning we were again leading by three runs, 11–8, a very small lead in slow-pitch softball. A hit followed two quick outs putting a man on first base. The next batter hit a high and long fly ball to right center field. Already playing deep, I backed up and camped under the ball. It seemed like it took a long time for the ball to come down. I had time to happily recognize my improvement since the beginning of the season: nothing wobbled! I reached up with both hands and clamped the ball firmly in my mitt. I fielded the last out of the season! I'm keeping the ball.

Undefeated as a manager, I dutifully gathered our T-shirts, except one. Tim modestly refused to leave the field bare-chested, saying, "Who would want this shirt anyway?" Norm showed up during the second game to cheer for us. He reported that he was black and blue from ankle to butt. Norm refused our requests to show us.

Collecting our T-shirts gave me an opportunity to express my thanks to each of my teammates with a heartfelt hug. As I approached each teammate I was greeted by an outstretched hand for a handshake. But I'm a hugger. To my delight, my hugs were matched by equally strong and warm embraces. We said goodbye not with sadness, but with a joyful sense of accomplishment and participation in a team experience. I will wash and fold these T-shirts with care and dedication, fulfilling the trust placed in me by Coach Bill.

EPILOGUE

We were reluctant to leave after our last game. Suddenly we had to confront the fact that we wouldn't be seeing each other until next year. And next year depends on so many things: continuing good health, world conflicts, earthquakes, the economy ... problems and possibilities from which we found escape on a softball diamond. I was thinking that throughout our country similar scenes were taking place and that many older men had experienced a softball season like mine. It was a heart-warming thought.

Throughout the season, I noticed a behavior among my teammates that is endearing. It took a few games to register on me, but then I delighted in observing this common reaction. When a teammate is complimented, "good hit, good play, or good catch," the response is consistent and universal among the players. First there is a boyish, small smile and then a quiet thank you. It is a very gentle moment, a stop in time acknowledging all the emotions and thoughts that have brought us to this softball diamond. Some of my teammates have had a long career in either baseball or fast-pitch softball, competing at a very high level, and yet there is a humbleness that accompanies this recognition by a teammate. Every one of us recognizes that making a good hit or play at this stage in our lives is really something special, and it requires a quiet savoring, with gratitude for health good enough to allow playing ball. There is a silent satisfaction that "I can still do this!"

I love these guys. Maybe we wouldn't be close friends in a different environment, and surely our politics would differ, but on a ball field we shared the uplifting camaraderie that can be found only in playing a team sport. I am grateful for the patience and support provided by my teammates in helping me to return to softball after a hiatus that had to be measured in decades. I am sad to have the season end. Maury gave me some perfect season-ending words: "I would love to be a team member with you next year."

SEE YOU
**next
year...**

REFERENCES

Prologue

1. **National Slow Pitch Softball History Home Page,** *www.angelfire.com/sd/slopitch/history.html*, May, 2006.
2. **Liberman N.,** *Glove Affairs. The Romance, History, and Tradition of the Baseball Glove,* Triumph Books, Chicago, 2003, p. 14.
3. Ibid., p.25.
4. Ibid., p.28.
5. **Russell D.A.,** What Happens When Ball Meets Bat?, *http://www.kettering.edu/~drussell/bats-new/ball_bat-0.html*, May, 2006.
6. **Kirkpatrick P.,** Batting the Ball, *Am J Phys* 31:606-613, 1963.
7. **Ashley S.,** Getting Good Wood (or Aluminum) on the Ball, *Mechanical Engineering:* pp. 40–47, October 1, 1990.
8. **Cross R.,** The Sweet Spot of a Baseball Bat, *Am J Phys* 66:772–779, 1998.
9. **Cross R.,** The Bounce of a Ball, *Am J Phys* 67:222–227, 1999.
10. **Nathan A.M.,** Dynamics of the Baseball–Bat Collision, *Am J Phys* 68:979–990, 2000.
11. **Nathan A.M.,** Characterizing the Performance of Baseball Bats, *Am J Phys* 71:134–143, 2003.

12. **Koenig K., Mitchell N.D., Hannigan T.E., Clutter J.K.,** The Influence of Moment of Inertia on Baseball/Softball Bat Swing Speed, *Sports Eng* 7:105–117, 2004.
13. **Adair R.K.,** *The Physics of Baseball,* Third Edition, Perennial, New York, 2002, p.33.
14. **Nathan A.,** Baseball — Gold Glove Page, *http://www.npl.uiuc.edu/~a-nathan/pob/evolution.html*, May, 2006.
15. **Baseball,** *http://www.madehow.com/Volume-1/Baseball.html*, May, 2005.
16. **Bealle M.A.,** *The Softball Story,* Columbia Publishing Company, Washington, D. C., 1957, pp.1–13.
17. **Dickson P.,** *The Worth Book of Softball. A Celebration of America's True National Pastime,* Facts on File, New York, 1994, pp.46–54.
18. **Adair R.K.,** *The Physics of Baseball,* Third Edition, Perennial, New York, 2002, p.149.
19. **Liberman N.,** *Glove Affairs. The Romance, History, and Tradition of the Baseball Glove,* Triumph Books, Chicago, 2003, p. 39.
20. Ibid., pp.62,63.

Umpiring

1. **Dickson P.,** *The Worth Book of Softball. A Celebration of America's True National Pastime,* Facts on File, New York, 1994, p. 146.
2. Ibid.

BIBLIOGRAPHY

Books

1. **Adair R.K.,** *The Physics of Baseball,* Third Edition, Perennial, New York, 2002.
2. **Bealle M.A.,** *The Softball Story,* Columbia Publishing Company, Washington, D.C., 1957.
3. **Dickson P.,** *The Worth Book of Softball. A Celebration of America's True National Pastime,* Facts on File, New York, 1994.
4. **Liberman N.,** *Glove Affairs. The Romance, History, and Tradition of the Baseball Glove,* Triumph Books, Chicago, 2003.
5. **United States Specialty Sports Association,** *2005 Official USSSA Slow Pitch Playing Rules and By-Laws,* United States Specialty Sports Association, Kissimmee, Florida, 2005.

Articles

1. **Ashley S.,** Getting Good Wood (or Aluminum) on the Ball, *Mechanical Engineering:* pp. 40-47, October 1, 1990.
2. **Cross R.,** The Sweet Spot of a Baseball Bat, *Am J Phys* 66:772–779, 1998.

3. **Cross R.,** The Bounce of a Ball, *Am J Phys* 67:222–227, 1999.
4. **Kirkpatrick P.,** Batting the Ball, *Am J Phys* 31:606–613, 1963.
5. **Koenig K., Mitchell N.D., Hannigan T.E., Clutter J.K.,** The Influence of Moment of Inertia on Baseball/Softball Bat Swing Speed, *Sports Eng* 7:105–117, 2004.
6. **Nathan A.M.,** Dynamics of the Baseball–Bat Collision, *Am J Phys* 68:979–990, 2000.
7. **Nathan A.M.,** Characterizing the Performance of Baseball Bats, *Am J Phys* 71:134–143, 2003.
8. **Thurston B.,** It's a Different Game. Aluminum Bat Performance vs. Wood Bat Performance, *Baseball Res J*, January 1, 2003.

Internet Sources

1. **Baseball,** *http://www.madehow.com/Volume-1/Baseball.html*, May, 2005.
2. **Nathan A.,** Baseball — Gold Glove Page, *http://www.npl.uiuc.edu/~a-nathan/pob/evolution.html*, May, 2006.
3. **National Slow Pitch Softball History Home Page,** *www.angelfire.com/sd/slopitch/history.html*, May, 2006.
4. **Russell D.A.,** What happens when ball meets bat?, *http://www.kettering.edu/~drussell/bats-new/ball-bat-0.html*, May, 2006.

INDEX

Compiled in love by Dick Colbeth, — "I'll run my own bases if you don't mind, thank you very much, Coach."